STOKE HAMMOND YESTERYEAR
A Personal Record 1925-1948

Stoke Hammond Yesteryear
has been published
as a Limited Edition
of which this is

Number **209**

A list of original
subscribers is printed
at the back
of this book

FRONT COVER: Stan Andrews, the baker from Soulbury stands outside Bonner's with his baker's cart. Assisting him is Raymond Kirk, who was in the author's class at school.

Stan Andrews, the baker from Soulbury stands outside Bonner's with his baker's cart. Assisting him is Raymond Kirk, who was in the author's class at school.

STOKE HAMMOND YESTERYEAR
A Personal Record 1925-1948

BY

MARGARET AITKEN

BARON
MCMXCVII

PUBLISHED BY BARON BIRCH FOR QUOTES LIMITED
AND PRODUCED BY KEY COMPOSITION,
SOUTH MIDLANDS LITHOPLATES,
CHENEY & SONS, HILLMAN PRINTERS (FROME) LIMITED,
AND WBC BOOK MANUFACTURERS

© Margaret Aitken 1997

All rights reserved. No part of this publication may be reproduced, stored in a retrieval system, or transmitted, in any form or by any means, electronic, mechanical, photocopying, recording or otherwise, without the prior permission of Quotes Limited.

Any copy of this book issued by the Publisher as clothbound or as a paperback is sold subject to the condition that it shall not by way of trade or otherwise, be lent, re-sold, hired out or otherwise circulated without the Publisher's prior consent, in any form of binding or cover other than that in which it is published, and without a similar condition including this condition being imposed on a subsequent purchaser.

ISBN 0 86023 564 5

Contents

Acknowledgements	6
A Railway Family	8
Track and Field	18
Water, Water Everywhere	30
Shop!	44
Learning the Hard Way	48
On the Right Road	58
Songs and Sundays	64
Fun and Games	72
Off to Work	76
The War Years	80
Here and There	88
Home from Home	92
Index	98
Subscribers	100

ACKNOWLEDGEMENTS

I would like to thank the *Bletchley Gazette* and *North Bucks Times* for the reproduction of several photographs. Every effort has been made to trace copyright holders. Thanks are also due to the staff of the *Leighton Observer* for their help in trying to trace photographers.

My sincere thanks go to Mary Bonner, Gerald Denchfield, Keith Gadsden, Malcolm and Peter Garner, Eileen Green, Pauline Gillham, John Harrup, Sheila Hyde, 'Bill' Kirk, Nellie Kirk, Flo Scott, Les and Roland Shepherd, Irene Robinson, Gwen Simmons, Joan Simmons, Kath Smith, Ivy Wood and Audrey Yorke for lending me their precious photographs to illustrate my book — and what would I have done without Hazel Turner, who had the unenviable job of typing my manuscript — thank you, Hazel!

Last, but by no means least, grateful thanks go to my daughter, Alison Davies, without whose help and encouragement I might have given up.

ABOVE: The shop built by the Bonners in 1927, with the Gilbert Scott telephone box demolished by a lorry in 1977 after a fatal accident with a tractor, when farm-girl Gill Adcock was killed. BELOW: These two cottages, now demolished, housed Mr and Mrs George Simmons and Miss Annie Green.

The 'old' Shop, once a Baptist Church, with the author's mother, Elizabeth Bonner, and wholesaler Len Bushell of Fenny Stratford. The author is the smallest child, pictured with her cousin Bess Scott, a young friend, and another cousin, Harold Scott, leaning against the wall.

A RAILWAY FAMILY

One could be forgiven for never having heard of Stoke Hammond but it is a pretty little north Buckinghamshire village south of the Milton Keynes conurbation, tucked in-between two local towns, Bletchley and Leighton Buzzard.

A continuous stream of traffic roars through the modern village — but it was not always like this. As I walk through today's Stoke Hammond I sometimes look across the village green towards the little old shop where I was born. My eyes stray to the bedroom window where one Sunday afternoon in January 1925 I first saw the light of day. Older residents have since told me they remember when I was born, how they had been on their way to the evening service at Chapel when they heard the news.

The Wesleyan Chapel in Chapel Yard was no more than a stone's throw from our shop. A footpath along the edge of the green led to it. Back in 1925 plans were already afoot to build a new Chapel away from the centre of the village in Newton Road. At the same time my parents were also planning to build a new house and shop, still overlooking the green but from a different angle.

In due course work began on both projects and in October 1927, with much excitement and celebration, the new Chapel and the new shop were opened on the same day.

Across the green and to the right of the old shop, two little cottages once stood, where old Mr and Mrs Simmons and their neighbour Annie Green lived. I can still picture them in my mind's eye. Now, three council bungalows stand on the piece of land and it occurs to me that I do not know anyone who lives in them.

To the left of the old shop still stands Rose Brook Cottage, looking much as it did when I was a child. In those days my best friend lived there with her mother, father and older sister. Enid is my age, and her father Will Scott was first cousin to my mother. Enid had a fair complexion and shoulder-length wavy blond hair. Her Grandpa Scott and my Grandpa Scott were brothers and both lived in the village with their large families, along with another brother and his family. There were a great number of Scotts living in Stoke Hammond, all Methodists. Enid and I were inseparable. We played together and went to the same school and Sunday School.

When we were about seven years old Enid told me her family were moving to Northampton.

Even at that young age I felt devastated. I pleaded with her not to go.

'We've got to, Dad's going to work there,' she answered, quite matter-of-factly as though she was looking forward to the move!

'Tell him you don't want to. Tell him you want to stay here,' I begged almost in tears.

'I've got to go!' was her final word on the subject.

Her Dad worked on the railway, as did my Grandpa and hers and practically all our uncles and male cousins. I grieved when Enid had gone — but I could not contemplate life without a best friend, so immediately set about finding another.

Jean Simmons, an only child, was our age too. She lived in a house called Rose Bank opposite the school and did not seem to have a special friend so I decided to ask her.

'Now Enid's gone away, will you be my friend?' I asked, straight to the point.

'All right!' she said, in a tone that seemed to indicate she did not care one way or the other.

'Like me and Enid were,' I persisted.

'Yes, all right, if you like,' she said. It was a binding promise which we both kept, we remain close friends to this day.

A slow-moving tractor lumbers up the road behind me, interrupting my reverie. When the road is clear I cross over and stand beside the Shepherds' garden wall. Old Mr and Mrs Shepherd and their two sons lived in the cottage when I was a child. The two boys, Les and Frank, were quite a few years older than me but I was fond of them. I also liked Mrs Shepherd a lot. Her grandson now lives in the cottage.

Leaning against the wall I can see the cottage where my grandparents lived, and joined onto it the cottage where my great-grandparents also lived.

Grandma and Grandpa owned the left-hand cottage and even now from the outside it looks much the same. The cottage had two rooms downstairs with a railway sleeper barn built onto the back. This was known as the 'wash-'us' and behind the door was a sink on a wooden stand holding a chipped enamel washing-up bowl. On a ledge behind it were two pieces of soap: red carbolic and white Sunlight. The red was used to wash hands and faces and the white was for washing clothes.

The living-room was small and dark with only one window. Opposite the shining, black-leaded grate was a row of doors. Behind the first was the pantry. The second hid the stairhole cupboard and was as black as ink inside. The last door secreted the wooden staircase. At the top of the stairs a landing-cum-bedroom was just large enough to hold a bed. The two other rooms, through which you had to walk to reach the furthest, held double beds. My grandparents brought up eight children in this small cottage.

George was the oldest son and worked for the railway, in the boiler sheds at Bletchley Junction. I loved his wife, Auntie Daisy, as she would let me do almost anything.

My mother, Elizabeth, known as 'Our Liz', came next. Being the eldest daughter, she was almost like a second mother to her younger brothers and sisters. Liz had wavy auburn hair, which unfortunately none of us inherited. After leaving school she went into service.

Fred, the second son and named after his father, had a gentle nature like Grandpa. He too worked on the railway, as a traindriver.

Minnie, the second daughter, came next — she lived to see her hundredth birthday. Because she did not go out to work but stayed at home to help in the house she was allowed to have piano lessons and became a music teacher. She married a local boy named Joe Keen, who, of course, worked on the railway as an engine driver.

Tom came next in line. He had straight auburn hair and after he married, lived for many years in Bedford. He too became an engine driver.

Auburn-haired Florence — 'Flo' — was next. She broke with tradition by marrying a coal merchant, Albert Sharpe. He had a house and a coal-yard at Bletchley and in later years bought a furniture van and did removals.

Arthur, the youngest son, married later on in life and I remember him as a bachelor living at home with Grandma and Grandpa. Arthur became a ganger on the railway like his father.

The baby of the family was christened Winifred but was known as Win. She married a village boy named Arthur Barron, who also worked on the railway. He became an inspector and all his adult life was a Methodist local preacher.

As a ganger, Grandpa supervised a gang of men who were responsible for the upkeep of two miles of track running on an embankment through fields at the back of village. At weekends Grandpa had to walk the two-mile stretch to make sure there was no subsidence and that the track was in good repair. During foggy weather it was his job to see that detonators were placed on the rails, which, when a train passed over them, went off with a loud bang. This alerted the driver to slow down, then stop.

The railway gang also cut and burnt the banks in a controlled way, encouraging wild flowers and grasses to grow year by year. Now that the track has been electrified the banks have become overgrown with shrubs, brambles and, in some cases, trees.

More memories flood back as I look towards the 'new' shop. I was two years and nine months old when we moved there. The double-fronted building still looks about the same as when it was my home. The only difference is the shop-door entrance, which has been altered a little for easier access. Three little cottages used to stand to the left of the shop and in the first one lived Enid's grandparents, my great-uncle Jim and great aunt Emma. I often visited them with my friend. Now one modern house stands in its place.

'Hello Margaret! Nice day!' calls a voice from across the road.

'Yes, it's lovely,' I reply, slightly startled and feeling just a little guilty, 'You caught me day dreaming'. My friend laughs as she makes her way down the road. I take the hint and walk up the hill towards home.

Rose Bank, opposite the 'old' School, where the author's 'new' friend Jean Simmons lived.

ABOVE: The 'old' Shop photographed in 1996 showing Rose Brook cottage where childhood friend Enid lived with her parents Will and Vi Scott, and her older sister Madge. BELOW: The cottage where grandparents Frederick and Sarah Scott lived is on the left, adjoining Uncle George and Auntie Daisy's cottage. The tall poplar tree was felled to make room for the Bonners' retirement bungalow.

Grandma Scott stands at the door of her tiny cottage, where she brought up eight children.

LEFT: Grandfather Frederick Scott. RIGHT: Aunt Minnie Keen lived to be over one hundred. BELOW: The Slad railway arch shows part of the length where Grandpa Scott was Ganger.

ABOVE: The Green, with seat and chestnut tree presented by the Gale family in memory of their son Robert, killed in 1944, and the telephone kiosk demolished in the accident. BELOW: The cottages, now demolished, where Great Uncle Jim and Aunt Emma lived. The thatched house was once the Post Office, and previous to that the Bell Inn, demolished to make way for a small estate named Olde Bell Close.

ABOVE: Houses and bungalows make up Olde Bell Close. BELOW: Little Thatch, opposite the Methodist Church.

LEFT: Tom Kirk in front of the old barn, and RIGHT: taking a breather: Arthur Kirk at Moat Farm. BELOW: Moat Farm (1966) showing the end of an original cowshed.

TRACK AND FIELD

The LMS Railway was one of the main sources of employment of the men of Stoke Hammond. Not all worked locally on the village length: some cycled to Bletchley Junction where they did a variety of jobs. Several were porters who assisted passengers with their luggage. Those who were guards made sure that doors were properly closed and platforms clear before blowing their whistle.

The firemen worked on the footplate shovelling coal. Others worked in the locomotive sheds on repairs. Some were signalmen, responsible for making sure that the track was clear, while still more shunted carriages and trucks in the siding.

Although working on the railway Mr Shepherd had a different job. He drove a horse and trolley around Bletchley and the surrounding villages, delivering goods that had been dispatched by rail. Usually, on a Saturday morning, he drew his horse to a standstill in front of our shop. On the cart would be boxes, packages and sometimes a large slatted wooden crate stuffed with straw which had come from the Potteries. Dad and Mr Shepherd gently slid the crate down planks of wood onto the ground to be unpacked. Inside there would be jardinieres in all sizes, colours and designs, pretty china teasets, washstand and dressing-table sets, vases and ornaments. It was fascinating to watch each layer reveal something more beautiful than the last. Many a sale took place before the goods actually reached the shelves. When everything had been priced and stacked away, the straw was bundled back into the empty crate and I was encouraged to jump on it to push it down. When the job was completed the crate stood in front of the shop until Mr Shepherd called again with his horse and trolley to collect it.

The next important source of employment in the village was farming. At least 16 farms were being worked. Some were owner-occupied; others rented land. A number of farmers with large acreages employed labourers and at haytime and harvest hired casual workers for the season. Each farm had its herd of milking cows, pigs, sheep and poultry, together with some arable land.

On the bend of the road coming into the village from Leighton Buzzard was Moat Farm, where two brothers named Tom and Arthur Kirk farmed. They lived side-by-side, overlooking the farmyard, and between them had 10 children.

Opposite Moat Farm was Mount Pleasant, farmed by Fred Adams. The farm has changed hands many times since then and various fields have been sold off to different buyers. One near the road now has eight luxury four- and five-bedroom houses built upon it.

Opposite Mount Pleasant is Bridge Farm, which is on the far side of the brook. When I was a child Mr and Mrs Frank Gale lived there. Their son Robert was killed in action during World War II and his name is listed on the roll of honour in the Parish Church. Once again the land has been sold off to several different people.

Fifty yards up the road is Brook Farm, which belonged to Tom Simmons, Jean's uncle. His cows supplied the village with milk. Every morning before going to school I went to the farm with four cans to collect milk for Grandma, Auntie Daisy, Auntie Win and my mother. The cans each held three pints and I carried two in each hand. A silver milkchurn stood under a lean-to shed. Resting on top of it was a muslin straining cloth and above it on the wall was the milk tank and cooler. Mr Simmons would tip a bucket of warm frothy milk straight from the cows into the tank, turn on the tap, and the creamy white liquid flowed over the cooler, through the strainer and into the churn. On the side of the churn hung the one pint and half pint measures.

Depending how much milk was required the amount was tipped into my cans, usually by Mrs Simmons. We paid for it at the end of the week. I was given 2d (old money) per week by my relatives and this money was saved until I had enough to buy a 15 shilling National Savings Certificate at the Post Office kept by Ivy Shepherd.

Papermill Farm at the far end of Bragenham Side was farmed by Arthur Bone. The road to it was narrow and in places passed between grassy banks. That was before the council houses and bungalows were built and, later, the new school.

Although Papermill is actually in the parish of Soulbury we considered it to be one of our farms. Bragenham Side continued on over the Turnover bridge, which spanned the Grand Union Canal, until it reached the river beside which the farmhouse is situated, about a quarter of a mile further on. In those days, after a lengthy spell of rain the river flooded badly so that at times the farm was cut off from the village.

Will Simmons, Jean's Dad, also had fields bordering the river and canal. Around them were some of the best blackberry hedges in Stoke Hammond. Jean's Dad had use of the farmyard and buildings behind Bridge Farm and, as mentioned before, lived in the house opposite the school.

Central to the village is Tyrells Manor, then farmed by Mr Holmes and his son George. The manor house is large and square and set back from the road on top of the hill. It has changed hands many times in my lifetime and has been modernised. Once again, the fields have been sold off and an estate of houses has now been built where the old farmbuildings used to be.

Next to the Methodist Chapel in Newton Road is the house where Jean's Uncle 'Jack' lived. On the site of his farmyard and buildings two modern houses now stand. Mr Simmons owned more land further up Newton Road on the far side of the railway bridge.

Also on the other side of the railway bridge was another smallholding, called Spoil Bank. Two agricultural cottages, reached by a footpath across a field, stood back to back. A farmworker lived in one of the cottages and went to work at Grove Farm by means of a field bridge across the railway. Ernie Penny farmed the 20 acres belonging to Spoil Bank and lived in the cottage facing the road. In due course the old cottages were sold and pulled down to make way for two new houses.

Dorcas Farm came next. This was reached via Dorcas Lane, which is opposite the entrance to Spoil Bank. Again, the farm has changed hands many times but is one of the few still being worked.

Back on the main road again and down the hill towards Newton Longville is Common Farm, where Mr and Mrs Charlie Line and their two daughters lived. The house was situated across two fields but sadly is no more. A neighbouring farmer bought up the land and it is still in cultivation. A quarter of a mile up the same road stands Rectory Farmhouse. This farm now belongs to Mr and Mrs Andrew Gurney, who continue to work the land.

Chadwell Farm is situated off the Drayton Road and the farmhouse is reached by means of a track across two fields. Some of the land borders the railway embankment. The Phillips family have lived there many years and this too is a busy working farm.

Back in the village, and off Newton Road, is Church Road where I live. Opposite my house was a smallholding called The Laurels. It was farmed by Mr Fountaine, an elderly gentleman. The house has recently changed hands again.

At the top of Church Road and to the left of the Anglican church is Grove Farm. Most of the fields have been sold off to individual buyers. My memory is of Mr and Mrs Gadsden and their five children living there. We were all friends and at times Jean and I played at the farm with them.

At the east end of the church and bordering the churchyard is farmland and buildings owned by the Church Commissioners. This is rented by John Richardson, whose father before him also farmed the land.

Outside the village, heading towards Bletchley, is Southlands, then owned and farmed by George Simmons (a bachelor) and his two unmarried sisters, Kate and Ethel. Jean's uncle and aunts lived in the house that stands back from the road. In recent years the property has been sold and the fields split up and sold to individual people, some of whom keep horses and sheep.

The last farm in the confines of the village was Dairy Farm, owned and farmed by Charles Penny with the help of his daughters. The fields bordered the river and canal and in winter often became flooded.

The majority of residents of Stoke Hammond are independent and apparently prosperous people who own their own cars and houses. Some work locally in the towns of Bletchley and Leighton Buzzard while others work in Milton Keynes. Commuters travel to London by train, which only takes 35 minutes now. In the days of steam the journey took an hour. They work at a wide variety of jobs embracing many different occupations and professions. Gone are the days of farming and the railway as a main source of employment, and gone, too, is that era.

This new estate, named Mount Pleasant, was once farmed by Mr Fred Adams.

ABOVE: Brook Farm: Tom Simmons is entering with his wife Elsie Simmons, and an unknown man. The thatched portion has now caved in. BELOW: Bridge Farm cottages and Bridge Farm House.

ABOVE: The Olde Bell Inn on the village green — at one time the Post Office. BELOW: Papermill Farm and the river (1996).

ABOVE: Tyrells Manor, with Ethel Collyer. BELOW: Side view of Tyrells Manor with new houses where old farm buildings used to be.

ABOVE: Laurel Farm House was once farmed by Mr Fountaine. BELOW: St Luke's, the Anglican Church.

ABOVE: An unusual photograph of St Luke's taken from the field at the back of the Church. BELOW: The stained glass window in the Anglican Church was restored in 1931. At the bottom left hand corner St Luke's Church is depicted. (Photograph by Trevor Green and Victor Yorke)

ABOVE: The Old Rectory at haymaking time, believed to have been built in 1702 and said to be haunted. In the foreground, the tractor and hayturner belong to Mr Gadsden. BELOW: The Fordson Major tractor at the back of Grove Farm House — once driven by the author.

ABOVE: Grove Farm House, where the Gadsden family lived. BELOW: Swan Cottage, where Great Uncle John Scott lived.

ABOVE: The brook enters the village beside Moat Farm. The road was narrow and the thatched cottages were demolished years ago. BELOW: The brook in 1996, taken from nearly the same position, shows Mount Pleasant housing estate where the thatched cottages used to be.

Water, Water Everywhere

The brook that flows through the lower part of Stoke Hammond enters the village on the bend of the road by Moat Farm, where it does little to enhance the area because of the overgrown watercourse and banks. But it was not so in my childhood days. The stream then ran clear and clean and we would scoop up a handful of water to drink when we were thirsty. It swirled under the road bridge, making a mini-whirlpool, and chattered pleasantly over the stones on its way to the river.

The main watercourse flows under the road bridge into Bragenham Side, where it is met by another brook coming down from the Slad Fields. Both the Meadows and Slads were farmed by the Kirk brothers. Until its course was widened and straightened behind the houses bordering the village green the second brook overflowed regularly in winter. Properties overlooking the green were sometimes under two or three feet of water.

Villagers who cycled to Bletchley to work had to push their bicycles along the canal bank near Dairy Farm when the roads and fields flooded. A culvert under the canal either became blocked or could not cope with the volume of water.

In summer, when the days were warm, children took off their shoes and socks to paddle in the brook. Bending low, we crept under the bridges crossing it in search of minnows, bullheads and tiddlers, which we put into 2lb jam jars.

Another watery attraction was the village pond at the top of Church Road beside the Rectory wall. It was full of weeds and contained many newts. In our spare time we went newting there: you could see them swimming in the water or hanging onto the side wall. Having selected the newt to be caught, we used a stick and string to dangle a worm in front of it. When it made a grab we pulled it out and put it in a jar. All the newts went back into the pond again when we were ready to go home. Sadly, the pond was filled in many years ago and is now a beautifully mown patch of grass.

Before piped water was brought to Stoke Hammond people had to fetch their drinking water from wells and the village pump, which is still a feature, although not in use now. Dad used to fetch our drinking water in buckets from my grandparents' well 100 yards down the road. At home we had a soft water well in our backyard and on washing day and bath night we would lift off the cast iron lid and drop down the bucket on a rope, then haul up the water. The copper in the scullery was filled and the fire beneath it lit. On Mondays all the sheets, pillowcases, towels and so forth had a really good boil in Persil or Rinso. The copper stick kept the washing poked down so that the water did not boil over. Our washing line ran along the garden path parallel with the road, so everyone knew what we wore!

The Grand Union Canal runs through the outskirts of our village on the opposite side to the railway and in my young days was an important water highway. Barges plied up and down from the Midlands carrying heavy cargoes of coal and other merchandise. Uncomplaining horses pulled the boats along the cut, as it was called, tethered to the bows by long stout ropes. Occasionally a hoof would strike a flint, making you suddenly aware of the silent craft. The barges were steered and manned by weather-beaten bargees who often smoked clay pipes. Sometimes they would moor the boats at the Turnover bridge them walk up Bragenham Side to our shop. There they replenished their stock of groceries and bought twist tobacco to smoke and chew.

The One Lock, on the Fenny side of the Turnover bridge, had a lock-keeper named Cecil Harrup, who lived in a cottage close by. He wound up the paddles with a key to regulate the flow of water into and out of the lock. He also worked on repairs that needed doing and helped to cut the hedges bordering the towpath.

The Three Locks, on the Leighton Buzzard side of the Turnover bridge, was a lot more important and an interesting place to watch the boats go through. The lock-keeper, Bill Garner, had a busy job as there were side locks to control the water as well as the main canal locks. There still remains a wide basin where the barges passed or waited to go through the locks. Bill was a keen gardener and kept the surround immaculate and colourful with beds of flowers.

Not only was the canal a busy water highway but it was also our swimming pool! My Dad was the village swimming instructor. He could dive and swim like a fish. If Mr Bonner was going to be in charge parents were happy to allow their children to go to the canal. In his time Dad must have taught hundreds of people to swim — children and adults. Sometimes we met at the Turnover bridge and at other times we cycled along the towpath to the swingbridge. As its name implies, this bridge swung across a narrow part of the canal so that farmers could cross with their implements and cattle to fields on the other side. Jean's Dad had fields on the other side of the canal and, fortunately for us, always built his hayrick close to the swingbridge. This acted as our ladies' changing-room, behind which we dressed and undressed. Close to the bank the water was fairly shallow but it quickly dropped down to over six feet in depth. Some swimmers brought ready-inflated inner tubes which they swam in, played on and dived through. We always knew when a barge was coming as someone would notice that the water was moving and being drawn towards the lock which was out of sight. By the time the boat appeared we had almost forgotten, until along the towpath came the quiet horse — often with a nosebag. Those caught on the narrow path had to press themselves into the prickly hedge to let the animal by, while others sat on the bank and exchanged cheery greetings with the bargees. As the evening wore on and it was time to go home, learners and non-swimmers would ask Dad, 'Are you coming tomorrow, Mr Bonner?' 'Yes, if it's warm,' he would reply enthusiastically.

All this came to an end when the narrowboats were no longer needed for commerce and pleasure boats took their place.

In those far-off days we might have seen one lone fisherman on the bank. Now angling clubs use the canal most weekends, trampling down the grass verges and leaving litter behind. However, out of season the towpath is still a peaceful place to walk along, where nature can be seen at her best.

The brook runs in front of Brook Farm with a few houses in Phoebe's Orchard estate.

ABOVE: The green under flood water 1951, with Ivy Cottage and Rose Brook Cottage. BELOW: Looking down Church Road from the site of the village pond, (now filled in), Grove Farm Cottage is on the right.

ABOVE: Grove Farm Cottage 1996, with a house and bungalow standing on the site of the old thatched cottage.
BELOW: Mr George Barron gets his water from the village pump.

ABOVE: Another view of the pump shows Pump Cottage, Rothschilds Villa, and The Nook. BELOW: The pump as it looks in 1996. The houses have been modernised and extensions built on.

ABOVE: The Grand Union Canal — the Turnover Bridge and advertising for 'Real Food and Ale' at the Dolphin Inn. BELOW: Reflections in the canal at the One Lock where Cecil Harrup was Lock Keeper.

A booted Cecil Harrup with a workmate layers a hedge beside the towpath.

ABOVE: The Three Locks at Stoke Hammond — a busy and attractive place. BELOW: The Three Locks: some of the side locks.

ABOVE: The Pump House shows some of 'Bill' Garner's handiwork. BELOW: The Pump House in May 1996 — it has a new use now.

ABOVE: 'Bill' Garner, Cecil Harrup and workmates work on repairs to the lock. BELOW: The Three Locks public house and restaurant is a popular meeting place.

ABOVE: The Swing Bridge which farmers used to cross the canal. BELOW: What a difference 20-30 years make — the Swing Bridge as it looks in 1996.

ABOVE: 'Bill' Garner, The Three Locks keeper, who was a keen flower gardener. BELOW: Peace and quiet on the canal banks.

ABOVE: A well-known family outside their council house: Mrs Barron with her daughters Hilda, left, and Elsie, right. BELOW: The eight 'new' council houses, into one of which the Bonners moved in 1921, when they returned to Stoke Hammond from Australia.

Shop!

My father, 'Bert' Bonner, a Londoner, came to work for his brother Harry at Moat Farm (this was before the Kirk brothers lived there). Bert met and fell in love with Harry's housekeeper, Elizabeth Scott, and they emigrated to Australia where my sister Annis and brother Fred were born. Ten years later, in 1920, the family returned to my grandparents' tiny cottage in Stoke Hammond where room was made from them to live.

While Lizzie had been away in Australia her eldest brother George had married and produced two children. Bess was a little older than her cousin Annis, and Harold a little older than his cousin Fred. They lived next door to Grandma and Grandpa Scott. Somehow Bert and Lizzie, Annis and Fred squeezed into the already overcrowded cottage with Grandma, Grandpa and Lizzie's brothers and sisters who still lived at home!

Now that the Bonner family was back in the village Bert went to look for work and quickly found himself a job as a lorry driver for Jacobs Dairy. Early each morning he collected churns full of milk from farms around the locality, then repeated the collection in the afternoon. Annis was now five and a half years old so eligible to attend the village school with her cousin Bess. During the day Grandpa and his remaining sons and daughters went out to work, thus easing the overcrowding situation.

Fortunately eight new council houses were nearing completion in Fenny Road and within a few weeks the Bonner family was allocated one. For the next two years Bert worked at the Dairy, coming home for dinner at mid-day. Then rumour had it that the little shop on the green was for sale. Bert and Lizzie showed a keen interest and talked between themselves as to whether it would be a viable proposition to buy it. Although my grandparents were poor themselves, they promised their help and support in whatever decision Bert and Lizzie made. They took the plunge. They would buy the shop! The present owner, Mrs Tofield, sold a few essential groceries, sweets and paraffin oil. In due course the agreement was signed, money changed hands and the Bonner family moved into the house that was part of the shop. They now had the added responsibility of making a go of their own business.

In 1922 Bert bought a paraffin round for £50. This included a horse and cart and about 20 to 30 customers. In those days paraffin was the main source of fuel for heating, lighting and cooking. Most days Bert set off around the villages to serve his customers and look for new ones. His jovial personality and utter reliability spread by word of mouth until slowly but surely he was attracting more customers and reaching out to more villages, which meant travelling further and further afield.

Lizzie worked hard at home looking after the shop and bringing up her two children. There was little spare capital to replace stock each week. Often, on a Friday, she had to borrow money from her parents to pay the wholesaler's bill until Bert returned from the round with his takings. To supplement their income Lizzie made jam and pickles, which she sold in the shop. Bert was now visiting seven or eight villages within a radius of 15 miles. He had a few customers in Soulbury, Burcott and Wing — all of whom he served on the same day. Soulbury was a small village, Burcott not much more than a hamlet and Wing a bigger village with several shops. He also had customers in Newton Longville, Drayton Parslow and Stewkley.

Stewkley was a large village with several well-established shops, so Bert only called here and there with paraffin. On Friday he went to Dunton, Whitchurch and Oving, a journey of about 15 miles each way.

In spring, summer and autumn the round was most enjoyable. Bert loved being out of doors and having contact with so many different people. He was an extrovert and enjoyed every minute of it. Even in winter he rarely complained about the conditions. It was his job, and he knew that his customers depended on him for paraffin; more so in winter when the days were dark and there was snow on the ground.

Now that the round had expanded to more than double its size, with new customers being added most weeks, Bert felt they should take on an assistant. Lizzie's sister Flo, when asked, said she would like to help. She gave up her job in Bletchley and soon became a useful and valued member of the team, dividing her time between working in the shop and being out on the round.

Fridays, in winter, must have been a nightmare for them. Bert and Flo would rise in the early hours of the morning and, after breakfast, feed and water Darkie, the mare, then harness her to the cart. After lighting the paraffin side lights the two of them set off in the darkness with only a heavy waterproof horse-blanket wrapped around their knees. They would wear as many layers of clothes as was practicable, and Bert always wore boots and leather leggings buckled at the side. With enough food packed up for the day, Lizzie would stand at the shop door to watch them go. She listened to the crunch of the hard tyres on the wheels as the cart crossed the green onto the road then waited for the rhythmical clip-clop of the mare's hooves as it gathered speed, pulling the loaded cart away into darkness and silence.

Darkie knew her way along the twisting narrow road without much bidding. At the Three Locks Public House they turned right up to Soulbury and disembarked at the bottom of the steep hill to lighten the load for the mare. Around the village pond they turned right again to Stewkley. Journeying through the southern end of the village, they turned right towards Dunton. At the tiny village of Dunton work began. Although it was still fairly dark the people were about and the oil cans put out ready to be filled. On the far side of the village the narrow road ran through several gated fields so Flo had to open and shut the gates while Bert drove through. But they were now heading towards the large village of Whitchurch, situated on the main Buckingham to Aylesbury road. Whitchurch was a good village for customers. The people knew and liked 'Mr Bonner' for they knew they could always depend on him. At some houses they would be invited in for a cup of tea and be allowed to use the lavatory — situated in the back garden or yard. When the village had been served they travelled on to Oving. This also proved a good source of customers. By the end of a winter day they and Darkie were tired and leg-weary but now had the prospect of a long slow journey home, mostly in darkness. Each time they came to a steep hill, and there were quite a few to negotiate, Bert and Flo got off the cart and walked.

Lizzie, at home, would go frequently to the shop door to listen for the tired clip-clop of the horse's hooves and sigh with relief when at last she heard the familiar sound.

Darkie would be unharnessed from the cart and turned out onto the green to eat her fill of grass. She was such an intelligent little animal that when she was satisfied she set off along down the road and waited outside Tom Simmons' farm gate, where she was stabled at 2s 6d per week. Depending on the time of year, Dad would open the stable door and put her inside or turn her out into a paddock where she galloped around, delighted to be free of the cart. After the mare had been fed, watered and made comfortable for the night there was always a hot meal waiting on the table for the hungry tired pair. Annis and Fred, now growing up, had to help with any tasks they could do. With this concerted family effort the shop and round prospered and in 1924 I was conceived.

ABOVE: A group of Stoke Hammond children, taken in 1925. BELOW: Schoolchildren in 1913 with sisters Elsie and Hilda Barron — back row 2nd and 3rd from left.

Learning the Hard Way

The village green and its surrounding area has always invoked great affection in me, for I lived and grew up at the shop which overlooked it. There was no playing field in Stoke Hammond then and the shop and green, being central to the village, were where we children congregated.

The road, which ran beside the green, was a narrow and twisting B class road. The bends were acute and the gentle incline which now runs up by the side of the shop was once a steep hill. Only the fittest cycled up it. It was known as The Hill and still is by local people. Banks topped by hawthorn hedges with a good number of elm trees bordered the road before it was widened and straightened to gentle curves. The eight council houses where Mum and Dad first lived when they returned from Australia are on the right-hand side going towards Bletchley, but in the early 1930s another six were built opposite.

Back on the green, on the opposite side of the road was Mr Shepherd's barn wall, against which we spent many hours playing ball games. Naturally we stood in the centre of the road to do this. Occasionally the Kirks' horse pulling a farm cart might amble up to the Slad fields, or their herd of cows would block up the road as they sauntered from the Slads to Moat Farm at milking time. 'Cyclists coming down the hill moved a bit sharpish but had a bell and brakes. Those going up were in no hurry! There were a few pony and traps — Grandpa Scott had one — as well as a few horse-drawn delivery vans and a sprinkling of cars and motorbikes, but nothing very serious to disrupt our play.

At certain times of the year we girls played with our hoops and ran miles guiding them with a stick. Then there was the skipping season, but the game I enjoyed most of all was tops and whips. With no footpaths in those days the grass verges were usually soft enough to stick the top into. After decorating the top with coloured chalk or silver paper we would give it a whack with the whip and send it spinning into the road, marvelling at the patterns that evolved. While the boys were busy playing marbles and conkers we girls played hopscotch. The boys also played football on the green, making goal posts from two piles of coats. In summertime boys and girls played cricket and rounders. Through living at the shop everyone in the village knew me and I knew them. In those days I could have named every person living in every house.

This idyllic picture was marred by my infant/junior school days. To be objective, we got a sound education at the village school — but it was brought about by fear!

Our headmistress, Miss Munro, was notoriously strict. No one answered Teacher back and lived to tell the tale! No one went behind the woodshed without receiving the cane. Although small and petite, she ruled us with a rod of iron — or rather a wooden blackboard pointer.

Miss Munro lived in the school-house adjoining our classroom, between which there was a connecting door. Sometimes, before lunch, she would slip through to the house. Whatever the reason, she always posted a child out in front of the class. The said child was told to note down any talking, movement from seats or anything else not connected with lessons. When 'Miss' returned, Teacher's spy reported to her what had happened during her absence. Anyone who had misbehaved was called to the front and ordered to hold out his or her hand, then the cane whistled through the air and the unfortunate child, usually crying, returned to his or her seat.

I especially remember how on one occasion three or four boys were lined up in front of class waiting for their punishment. The first three received the cane and returned to their places. The last boy got his whack, then was stupid enough to smile. Teacher went beserk! 'I'll teach you to smile when you've had the cane,' she raged. 'Hold out both hands!' She then proceeded to give him six strokes, three on each hand. With bowed head and swollen throbbing hands tucked under his armpits he went back to his desk, but even then would not give her the satisfaction of making him cry.

In another incident two boys were caned across the back of the legs. The cane left large red wheals.

There was no such thing as truancy. We were terrified of the Attendance Officer, who came round frequently to inspect the register. If a pupil had been absent for any length of time the Attendance Officer went to the offender's home to investigate, and should a good reason not be forthcoming there was threat of prosecution.

Others who visited the school and also frightened us included the 'Nit Nurse', who looked through our hair and sent home any unfortunate child she discovered with head lice. The dentist, who happened to be female, was also a source of dread. Although she put a piece of cotton wool on the belt of the drill for us to watch, it did not fool us for one moment! We knew it was going to hurt.

Ours was a Church of England School and on Friday mornings the parson came to take assembly. He read from the Bible, led us in prayers and gave us long passages of scripture and psalms to learn by heart. When he came into the classroom we all stood up and, with a clatter of desk seats, chanted in unison 'Good-morning-Sir!'

It seemed ironic that the majority of us were brought up as non-conformists and went to the Methodist Sunday School and Chapel. At that time there were three main families in the village — the Scotts, to which I belonged — the Simmons, to which my friend Jean belonged — and the Kirks, with whom we played. All were staunch Methodists. Nonetheless, in accordance with the Anglican church calendar, on Saints' days and feast days we were marched up the hill to the musty and chilly church. Here the parson held a service before school commenced — a custom with which we Methodist children were familiar.

When we arrived at school each morning we stayed in the playground until Miss Munro came out to blow her whistle. At the first shrill whistle we stood perfectly still. The second blast sent us running to form two straight lines by the porch door, girls in one and boys in the other. Without a fidget or whisper, on the command 'Lead on' we filed into the cloakroom, taking off our coats and hats and hanging them on the appropriate pegs. When we had settled into our seats, Teacher took her place behind the high desk in front of class and called out our names from the register, to which we answered 'Yes Miss'. Next followed the morning hymn, prayer and scripture reading conducted by her.

We were well grounded in all the basic subjects — arithmetic and tables, reading, spelling, handwriting and composition. We studied history, geography, nature, music and did PE, which was called 'Drill'. While the boys did drawing and painting we girls were taught sewing. I enjoyed most of the subjects but my favourites were music, PE and nature study. Our nature tables was always full of interesting things we had taken to school and the high window ledges were loaded with jam jars of wild and garden flowers.

When the weather was fine we went into the playground for 'Drill'. This included team games, running, jumping, stretching and throwing bean bags. I enjoyed every minute of it and was an enthusiastic pupil. Singing lessons were also a delight, especially when I was given the second part of a song to sing.

When I was about seven years old I began to have private piano lessons with my school teacher. My older sister had lessons already but was not keen to practise and I really wanted to learn. Grandma and Grandpa Scott were keen for me to learn so that one day I might play the organ at Chapel, a wish dear to their hearts. Dad decided to ask Miss Munro if she would teach me privately: she agreed, and one Thursday after school I began.

It felt like punishment to have to stay behind when the other children had gone home — the classroom was big and empty and the clock on the wall ticked loudly. I felt lonely and apprehensive sitting on the high piano stool with my legs dangling in space. Miss Munro opened the notebook she had told Mum to get for me and wrote down the date, then propped up on the piano in front of me Ezra Read's first piano tutor. My musical education had begun. Although I had lessons with her until I went to senior school I never lost that butterflies-in-the-tummy feeling when I had to stay behind on Thursdays. Despite that, I have to thank my teacher for imparting her considerable musical knowledge to me, with the result that at the age of 12 years I *did* play the organ at Chapel — and continue to do so to this day.

The author's class in 1932: the tall girl in the centre is her friend Jean Simmons, and she is on her left.

ABOVE: The Old School and House. BELOW: The village green, where a pathway in front of the thick hedge led to cottages in 'Chapel Yard' and to the old Methodist Chapel — later to become the Village Hall.

ABOVE: The Kirks' horse. He pulled the farm cart up and down the road to and from the Slad fields. BELOW: Grandma and Grandpa Scott with a visitor in their pony and trap.

A group of young helpers assist Arthur Kirk at haytime.

ABOVE: The author plays the organ in the Methodist Chapel. She was first called on to play when about twelve years old. BELOW: The Old School House and part of the school in 1996. The house door, scattered with iron studs, is still the same one used by Miss Munro.

ABOVE: Schoolchildren are grouped around the maypole in the twenties. The author's brother, sister, and several cousins are in the photograph. BELOW: The class of 1928-29; brother Fred is back row 2nd from right.

57

ABOVE: Great Uncle Jim Scott — Sunday School Superintendent. BELOW: 1 Newton Road, the cottage where Mr George Bone used to live.

ON THE RIGHT ROAD

Once every village had its own roadmen — and Stoke Hammond was no exception. Albert Soulbury was a dumpy little man with a noticeable stomach and a considerable 'character'. He wore brown corduroy trousers held up by braces and a wide leather belt buckled around his middle, which usually slipped down somewhat. He was a hardworking, conscientious man who was always busy. Before there were curbstones and footpaths in the village, the grass verges were neatly chopped back, grassy banks were trimmed with the sickle and scythe and all waste was gathered up into the wheelbarrow and taken away. Likewise, on a Saturday morning the whole village was swept through and all loose gravel and grit was shovelled up and wheeled away. If the 'Best Kept Village' Competition has been in operation in those days we would have won it year after year.

In Newton Road there lived an old gentleman by the name of George Bone. Mr Bone had relatives living in Canada and every so often they would send him a batch of newspapers and comics, which he passed on to us. Enid and I would knock impatiently on his door to see if they had arrived. Then we were six or seven years' old and loved stories about fairies, totally believing in such creatures. One day when we asked Mr Bone if the comics had come he patted Enid on the head and called her 'fairy'. I was mortally offended that he did not call me 'fairy', but years later it occured to me that it was Enid's fair hair to which he was referring and not the winged variety!

Great-uncle Jim Scott was a lovely man with a smiling face and a kindly disposition. Whenever you saw him he was whistling a hymn tune. He owned two pieces of allotment ground on the outskirts of the village. One he used as a vegetable garden, while the other was an orchard, partly fenced off with wire netting, where his free-range hens scratched. On this piece of ground there were several sheds built with railway sleepers. One shed was special because there was a wooden seat outside; growing round the door were rambling red roses planted by him. Uncle Jim sat on the seat to smoke his pipe and meditate. Before he left the allotment field to return to the hubbub of the village he would pick a flower to put in his buttonhole. Then off he would go, whistling 'What a friend we have in Jesus'.

Mr and Mrs 'Billy' Rice were well-known village people, Mrs Rice, Enid's Aunt Em, had been a school teacher and also our Sunday

School teacher. She organised the Anniversary celebrations and Christmas concerts.

Mr Rice was a good singer and a very clever wheelwright who could make almost anything. In 1936 Dad got rid of the horse and cart and bought a 'gate change' Austin Ten car. On the chassis Mr Rice built our first motorised mobile shop. Behind the cab he constructed a wooden skeleton of four corner posts and a strong floor. The sides were left open and, in wet weather, could be covered by sail cloth curtains, which was fastened with hooks. Through the centre a space was left for the 50-gallon paraffin tank. This had a brass tap at the back and, suspended under it, Mr Rice had constructed a wooden box where the measures and funnels were kept. He built a series of shelves behind the cab, along the sides and over the top of the tank where Dad stacked his wares. Around the edge of the roof he added a little rail so that that space could also be used. Up there Dad stored door mats, coconut matting, bedroom and hearth rugs, galvanised iron buckets, enamelled washing-up bowls and chamber pots among other items. Hanging underneath from hooks by loops of string were handbrushes, fluebrushes, scrubbing brushes, broomheads, wet mops, polishing mops, dishcloths, floor cloths and milk jugs. They all swayed madly from side to side as the van travelled over bumpy roads, but I do not remember any major catastrophe.

Although our general store was the only shop in the village, Stoke Hammond was well supplied by a number of visiting traders. As well as selling paraffin, hardware and groceries, we also sold sweets, haberdashery and medicines. The latter were purchased from Wilfred Durrell, whose shop was at Leighton Buzzard. When not wearing his chemist's hat he was the local comedian and came to entertain us in a concert party. He sang humorous songs, told tales and kept us in fits of laughter.

The first trader that springs to mind was Stan Andrews, who came from Soulbury. Stan made his own mouth-watering crusty bread and brought it around the village in his high-backed baker's cart. His little pony stepped out at a fair rate of knots. He also made calorie-laden dough cakes and lardy cakes.

Mr White was the greengrocer from Wing, a village about five miles away. He came by cart on Friday afternoons with a colourful display of fruit and vegetables, especially bright yellow bananas and red rosy apples. Pomegranates, when they were in season, were a favourite. When cut in half they revealed fleshy seeds to be picked out individually with a pin.

Mr Lovatt cycled from Stewkley, and on the carrier of his bike was tied a bundle of men's clothing wrapped in waterproof American cloth. When the string was untied thick flannelette and khaki working shirts were revealed. There were also long woollen underpants and woolly vests with sleeves, as well as a selection of long woollen socks, suspenders and braces. Although all these items of clothing were necessary they were not of much interest to me. But mention Miss Whitaker and I still get a sense of excitement at the wares she brought in her case.

In the early days Doris Whitaker cycled from Leighton Buzzard with the case strapped on behind her but, as the years passed, she graduated to a motorbike and sidecar, then a small van. She was a draper specialising in ladies' and children's clothes and if you asked for something she had not brought with her she would bring it next time. Miss Whitaker was welcomed into most homes in the village, especially before the Sunday School Anniversary, when we girls had new clothes. It was exciting looking through her case of beautiful dresses in wonderful styles and pastel colours. On top of that, she brought straw hats with matching ribbons. Customers who could not pay in full, could pay so much per week. Some were in debt to her for many years and it was said that she never did get all the money from others!

Finally, there was Mr Tibbles, the rag-and-bone man. Most householders kept a rag-bag and into it went clothes that were worn out and no longer of use. My friend Jean and I spent hours dressing up with the contents of the rag-bag. Imagine our fury when Mr Tibbles came round and Mum gave him the dressing-up clothes. It took ages to collect a new 'wardrobe' of interesting items.

Mr Tibbles cycled from Leighton Buzzard, arriving in the village on a Saturday morning with several large empty sacks; on a good day he left with bulging sacks. He was small in stature but his manners were impeccable. 'Good morning Missus,' he would say to my mother, 'I'm paying a good price for rabbit skins today — if you've got any!' We usually had. Uncle Arthur went rabbiting with a ferret around the fields and on the railway bank. He usually caught several, which he sold in the village. We had one most weeks. Nothing was wasted because the skin was hung to dry until Mr Tibbles came.

When I was a small girl I had a fairy-cycle, which I outgrew, so my parents began to look around for a larger second-hand bicycle for me. One day my mother decided to aks Mr Tibbles if he ever came across anything that would be suitable. He said that he would keep his eyes open. At last the day came when he arrived with my bicycle. It was certainly second-hand but I was the proudest child in Stoke Hammond when it came.

One day I had a particularly nasty attack of hiccoughs, which still

Dressed in the contents of the rag-bag — groom Jean Simmons, bride, the author, and bridesmaid Daphne Williams.

persisted after holding my breath and drinking water from the opposite side of a glass. Unexpectedly my mother said to me 'Mr Tibbles will have your bike back, you know?' She continued talking about Mr Tibbles and the bike until I was so alarmed that I forgot all about my hiccoughs. Then a smile spread across her face, 'Have your hiccoughs stopped?' Nearly in tears, I slowly nodded my head. Her arm went round my shoulders, reassuring me that my bike was for keeps! Next time I had hiccoughs she only had to mention Mr Tibbles and my bicycle and I was cured!

ABOVE: The first mobile shop was built on an Austin 10 chassis by Mr William Rice of Stoke Hammond. BELOW: This photograph shows the author's father 'Bert' Bonner serving customer Mrs Atkinson, (a London evacuee), at Drayton Parslow.

This old cottage previously stood on the site of the present Methodist Church; Mrs King is with her small son.

Songs and Sundays

In the schoolroom of Stoke Hammond Methodist Church hangs a framed plaque commemorating the names of 27 children who brought weekly contributions for the laying of a stone in the 'new' Chapel. My brother's and sister's names are recorded, as is that of my friend Jean, and I was always annoyed that mine was not — but I was too young and no doubt Mum could not afford it.

There was no Sunday School at the Anglican church then, and, in fact, not for many years afterwards — so most of the village children attended the Methodist Sunday School. There were two sessions: at 10.30 am (for an hour) and at 2 pm, after which we stayed on to the service which ended at 3.30 pm. We sat on forms in the schoolroom, and from an early age I played the harmonium for the hymns. The American organ in Chapel was pumped by a handle or pedalled by foot and was played by Nell Robinson. Nell's husband, Reg, sat on a chair and pumped wind into the organ; occasionally Nell would glare at him when he was not concentrating. It was an impressive-looking instrument, with two manuals and a lot of stops. I was fascinated by it and had a go whenever I got the chance.

Just before the afternoon service began the children filed into the Chapel, girls sitting in the front pews on the right and boys on the left. Uncle Jim sat at the far end of the front pew so that he could oversee both pews. Grandpa Scott sat in the pew behind the girls to keep an eye on us. Sometimes the sermons were long and boring so, to relieve the tedium, we would idly swing our legs backwards and forwards. Gathering momentum, it was only a matter of time before someone kicked the pew in front with a resounding 'crack'. This brought forth a 'Shsssh' from Grandpa. There were other times during the service when we were lulled into drowsiness — then, all of a sudden, the preacher would raise his voice and thump on the pulpit, making us nearly jump out of our skins. This prompted more stiffled giggles and earned us a poke in the back from Grandpa.

There were many events in the year to which we looked foward, and one of those was the Sunday School outing to Wicksteed Park, near Kettering. One, sometimes two, 'buses would pull up on the green and we would clamber aboard with our teachers and mothers. What excitement there was as we drove through the Park gates. On the right were swings, slides, round-abouts, seesaws and rocking equipment. We did not have any of these luxuries where we lived and could not decide what to go on first. The little train which ran around the perimeter was a great favourite. It circled the lake and cut across a small corner of it so that at this point there was water on either side. I was terrified, imagining that the train would come off the rails and we would be drowned. At the end of the day, tired but happy, we sang all the way home.

During the winter there were social evenings to be enjoyed, with games of Postman's Knock and Spinning the Breadboard. At Christmas we gave a concert, performing sketches and playlets, for which we dressed up.

But the big event of the year was the Sunday School Anniversary, which was celebrated on the second Sunday in May. About a month prior to the date we began practising for the festivities. There were new songs and recitations to learn. On the Monday of Anniversary Week a wooden platform was erected in front of the pulpit. Forms and chairs were placed in rows and that week we rehearsed our programme on the stage, encouraged by our teachers to speak out loudly so that we could be heard at the back.

On the Sunday, with the girls in new dresses purchased from Miss Whitaker and the boys in new suits with highly polished shoes and well-brushed hair, the morning service began at 10.30. The children sat in the front rows on the platform and behind us were the augmented choir, who had also been learning new music and attending final rehearsals. Our service followed at 2.30 pm. The Chapel would begin filling up at 2 pm and, while people were taking their seats, the children and the choir sang the music they had sung during the morning service. The Chapel was usually full before 2.30, with extra chairs being placed down the aisle. We sang rather absent-mindedly while watching the people come in. Some had solos and most had recitations to say, so it was all a bit nerve-racking. The teachers sat in the front pew to prompt and give confidence to those who needed it, but on the whole we enjoyed the tension. After tea we came back for the evening service at 6 pm. Again the Chapel and schoolroom would be packed out as we and the choir sang a different set of songs. It was wonderful when the congregation joined in the first and last well-known hymns and together we nearly lifted the roof.

Celebrations continued on the Monday when, as a reward for our hard work, a wonderful tea was prepared. After school we rushed up to the Chapel and burst into the schoolroom like a herd of hungry elephants. The long trestle table was covered by a snowy white cloth and on it were plates of cucumber, tomato and fish and meat paste sandwiches. There were assorted cakes and colourful jellies, all of which quickly disappeared. After tea we ran up Church Road to play in great-uncle John's field until the evening service at 7 pm. Uncle John, who also had a pony and trap, gave us rides around the village. The time flew by until 6 pm, when we had to go home, wash and change and be back at Chapel to perform our Sunday afternoon programme.

When we reached our teens some of us joined the church group who went round the village carol singing the week before Christmas. Dad sang bass, we had a couple of tenors, Nell Robinson and I sang alto, and we had several sopranos.

Dressed in our warmest clothes and carrying torches we met in the Kirks' farmyard at 6 pm. Some of the men were not home from work by then, but by the time we had reached the Dolphin Inn they had joined us. Arthur Barron, my uncle by marriage, would be one of the first to arrive, his Tilley lantern shedding sufficient light for us to see by. The others arrived one by one until we had a full choir. The object of our carol singing was to collect money for the National Children's Home and Orphanages, so two of the non-singers were delegated to knock at doors while the rest of us sang. With no loud televisions to distract them the occupants could always hear us and often opened their doors to listen and join in. The first evening we went to all the houses in the village, while the second evening we walked miles to visit all the outlying farms.

It was great fun chattering and walking arm in arm along the road in the darkness, but it was less pleasant when we had to cross a couple of muddy fields to reach a farmhouse. On the whole, people looked forward to our coming year by year and gave generously to the cause. It was always a great joy and relief when we reached Stoke House — about half a mile out of the village towards Bletchley. We were kindly invited into the House, which in the past had been owned by gentry, and, after making sure that our shoes were clean, were ushered into the large sitting-room.

There our eyes feasted on an enormous decorated Christmas tree, which sparkled and twinkled in the light. It was an impressive sight after the darkness outside. Our hosts joined in several carols as we sang for our supper, then hot mince-pies and coffee were served. It made a delightful and welcome interlude.

Now we had just two more farms to visit, Dairy Farm and Southlands. At Southlands we shone our torches enviously into the branches of their variegated holly trees, which always seemed to be laden with shiny red berries. We also nudged our companions and had a giggle when the beams of our torches picked out hens roosting in the tops of apple trees, well away from prowling foxes. In later years we drove around the outlying farms in cars, but it was much more fun when we walked.

ABOVE: A group of Sunday School children with their teachers Arthur Barron, left, and Guy Cox, right. The Junior Missionary Association Cup is held up by John Cox and Brian Scott. BELOW: The Methodist Church in Newton Road, Stoke Hammond, built in 1927.

ABOVE: A Methodist Church social occasion — note the uniformed young man, who was stationed at the RAF Wireless Station. BELOW: A group of Methodist friends enjoy an afternoon in the author's garden: left to right: Mrs Barrow, Mrs Chambers, Mr Gadsden, Mrs F. Scott, Mrs H. Cheshire, Mr A. Barron, Mrs M. Keen, Mrs Gadsden and Andy Aitken — taken in 1984.

ABOVE: A selection of fruit, flowers and vegetables decorated the Methodist Church for Harvest Festival in 1982. BELOW: Flower Festival arrangements celebrate the opening of the new kitchen extension in 1992.

ABOVE: A famous Methodist outing — how many people can you recognise? BELOW: Stoke Lodge — Mrs Bonner worked in service there when she first left school.

ABOVE: A group of WI members, taken in the Village Hall, 1954. BELOW: The Dolphin Inn where the cricket team went for tea.

FUN AND GAMES

When the old Methodist Chapel near the green was no longer used for worship it was sold and converted into a village hall. The building was gutted and a small piece of land at the back purchased to build an extension for kitchen and toilets. The inside was redecorated and a committee set up to run it. Small tables and chairs were purchased and now the residents of Stoke Hammond had their own meeting place.

In those days we made our own entertainment — and the village hall was where it happened. Every Friday evening for many years my father organised the weekly whist drive, which was always well attended. Most weeks there would be 10 or 12 tables occupied and he acted as Master of Ceremonies. Jean and I were keen whist players and cycled to Drayton Parslow, Great Brickhill and, sometimes, on a Saturday evening to the Scouts' hut at Leighton Buzzard, where we played as partners.

Then there were the village dances. The music was usually provided by just a piano and drums but we still managed to have a good time. There was a fair mix of Old Time and Ballroom dancing, both of which we enjoyed. The local boys congregated on one side of the hall while we girls whispered together on the other. The boys seemed reluctant to ask us to dance but we did not mind all that much because we danced together, and we were much less likely to have our feet trodden on!

Concerts of all kinds were staged in the village hall, sometimes by visiting concert parties and sometimes by local talent. A wobbly stage made up of trestle tables was erected and curtains hung across the front of it, with rickety steps leading onto the stage. We sometimes feared for the safety of the dancers as they performed their routine.

The village hall was used for all sorts of things, including wedding receptions — mine was held there. During the winter months various social evenings were arranged. These consisted of organised games, competitions and dancing, followed by refreshments. Money-raising events like jumble sales and Christmas bazaars were also held, as were evening classes. The Old Time, Ballroom and Country Dancing classes were always patronised to capacity.

The Women's Institute, founded in 1947, held their monthly meetings there, and a large proportion of village women attended. In those days there was an active drama group, which performed plays and sketches. There was also a WI choir, which gave concerts in the hall and entertained at local old people's homes.

Another organisation to use the village hall was the Parish Council, in which local councillors discussed the best way of providing services for the residents of Stoke Hammond. Now the Parish Council and all other organisations meet in the 'new' school, which was closed some years ago because of falling rolls. The old hall became derelict, but a member of the Kirk family has bought it and is now in the process of turning it into a dwelling-house.

On the sporting front, Stoke Hammond has always been an enthusiastic and competitive cricketing village. My father, brother, uncles and male cousins all played, as did many other village men and youths. The captain never had any difficulty in selecting teams for Saturday matches — it was more a case of who to leave out!

The cricket pitch was located in the Kirks' first meadow. It was protected by a removable wire fence, which prevented the herd of cows from wandering on to the green. The outfield was rough and at times quite hazardous, particularly in early summer when the cows had been grazing the new grass.

Looking over the five-barred gate on the bend of the road opposite Moat Farm, the distant pitch was bounded at the far end by the railway embankment and by the brook on the right-hand side. Sloggers had no difficulty in scoring a six when they hit the ball onto the railway bank or into the brook, from which some luckless fielder had to retrieve it.

On the left-hand side close by the hedge was a small wooden 'pavilion' built by Mr Rice. It served as a changing-room for the players and as a vantage point for scorers to record the progress of the match. One or two wooden benches were placed in front of the pavilion for older parishioners to sit on while the rest of us lounged on the grass. The only excessive noise was when a steam passenger train roared by on the railway track, or when a goods train clattered past in its own good time.

There was great rivalry between the village teams, and we girls had our favourites, based not so much on playing abilities as on individual players.

At half-time the players walked up the road to the Dolphin Inn where tea had been prepared for them. Spectators either picnicked or cycled home for theirs, returning later to support the home team.

ABOVE: Stoke Hammond cricket team: left to right: D. Stanesby, F. Bonner, G. Shackshaft, K. Murphy, D. Denchfield, F. Collins, C. Scott (umpire), J. Goodman, C. Hallwood, S. Kirk, B. Tearle, and R. Stanesby. BELOW: The football team: A. Shackshaft (referee), D. Denchfield, D. Stanesby, R. Emmerton, G. Denchfield, W. Kirk, G. Shackshaft, L. Sharman, D. Barker, G. Stanesby, B. Stevenson, and A. Aitken.

ABOVE: Aylesbury Road, Wing — where we started our rounds. BELOW: Little London, Whitchurch, where we finished.

OFF TO WORK

When World War II broke out in September 1939 we had left school and had found ourselves jobs — not at the same place because Jean was interested in office work and my mother dearly wanted me to become a dressmaker.

In nearby Fenny Stratford there was a draper shop called Cowlishaws, which took dressmaking apprentices. Apprentices had to do all the menial jobs for very low wages. In contrast, Jean was getting 5s per week at the Co-op. With dressmaking in mind, I was then pointed in the direction of the Rodex coat factory at Bletchley, which made high-class garments and paid 7s 6d per week.

Inside the factory were rows of electric sewing machines, which made a considerable din when they were all working. After the forelady had explained to me what I had to do, she gave me a piece of canvas interfacing to work on. It took me a little time to adjust to the speed, but eventually machining canvases became a doddle. My next step was making up coat linings. A ready cut-out bundle would arrive, often in beautifully coloured satin. When I had become experienced at making up linings I was then put onto coats. The material was of a high quality and at first I was only allowed to machine the seams. But later, when I had gained the required experience, I made up the whole garment in a variety of styles, some with top stitching. The next process was to learn how to make up and insert complicated pockets. I had just reached this stage of my career when I had to give in my notice and leave the Rodex coat factory for good.

Almost immediately after the outbreak of the war, my brother Fred, aged 20, had become one of the first militia men in the district to be called up into the Army. Fred normally worked at home with Dad. Most of the time was spent out on the round or filling up the van ready for the next day. My sister Annis still worked in the shop and the Post Office which he had now acquired, but Flo, Mum's sister, had married Albert Sharpe the coalman, so I had to take Fred's place at home.

My new job entailed working out on the round with Dad and serving in the shop and Post Office. I really enjoyed being out in the fresh air and getting to know the customers. Some were dear old souls who had dealt with us for years. I had to help Dad 'do' the van every time we came back from the round. This meant stacking the shelves with groceries and pumping the tank full of paraffin.

On Monday mornings at about 8.45 Dad would set off in the van for Soulbury, serving the outlying customers on his way. After the first rush of customers in the shop, I cycled after him and caught up just as he had begun serving in the village. With my bike propped up against a convenient wall or hedge, I then got down to work. I had my own customers to serve and Dad had his. Both Dad and I wore leather money bags across our shoulders, with coppers in the first section and silver in the second. I used to keep a few 10s notes for change but gave the £1 notes to Dad. Some of the housewives would come out to the van to look around and help themselves. Most of them wore a pinafore, which they would hold up with one hand to form a bag, into which they put items of shopping until we added up the contents. When we had finished at Soulbury, Dad went on alone to Burcott and Wing, where there were only a few customers, and I cycled home. After dinner I washed and changed and served behind the counter with my sister. When Dad came home from the round I had to pump the tank and help him 'do' the van.

Tuesday was our half-day closing and how we all looked forward to it. It was market day at Leighton Buzzard. In the early afternoon Dad got out the car and we all piled in. At Dixon's Garage he would fill up with enough petrol to last us through the week. When we had browsed around the stalls we then took on the shops. If we needed new clothes, shoes or knitting wool and jumper patterns this was the place to buy them. I loved rummaging around Purrett's Music Shop. It was dark, dingy and untidy inside, but I could usually find what I needed. If the required sheet music was not in stock Miss Purrett would order it and it would be there the next week. Annis and I enjoyed buying the latest songs that we had heard on the wireless. Sometimes, as an extra treat while we were in Leighton Buzzard, we stayed on for the pictures at the Oriel Cinema.

On Wednesday Dad went to Newton Longville on his own. He did not need my help as we did not have so many customers there, so I worked in the shop and Post Office.

We visited Drayton Parslow on a Thursday. Dad drove on ahead of me and I cycled later to catch him up. We had some nice customers there and one in particular I shall always remember. Her name was Mrs Harold Capp and she lived in one of the newer detached houses, with a well-kept front garden. One winter's day, when it was bitterly cold and my hands were frozen from drawing paraffin and carrying heavy cans, she invited me in. 'Come and have a warm by the fire,' she said. She took me into her best room, where she pulled up a pouffe and sat me down in front of the hearth. A while later she brought me a steaming cup of cocoa made with milk. I must have looked like an urchin in my dirty old working clothes and smelling strongly of paraffin. It is a wonder, though, that I had not ignited in front of the fire! After that episode I always thought of Mrs Capp as a real lady.

Friday was a long hard day, but, compared with the early days when Dad and Auntie Flo went off in the horse and cart, it was easy. We now had the mobile shop with a warm cab to protect us from the weather, but we also had a bigger round and more customers so it took almost as long. The sale of paraffin had greatly increased so that now we had to rendezvous in Whitchurch at mid-day with an oil tanker that came from the depot at Aylesbury to fill up the tank on the van. When we reached Little London Mrs Gurr would bring out a tea tray, set with cups and saucers, a jug of milk, sugar and a pot of tea covered by a cosy. We drank this with our packed lunch.

In the early afternoon we continued on to Oving, which adjoins Whitchurch. We did not have quite so many calls there but it still took several hours. When the last customer in Oving had been served we tightened up the remaining depleted stock, unrolled the canvas side-curtains and hooked them in place ready for the journey home. By now we were tired, but satisfied with a good day's work well done. Once we were out in the countryside Dad would hand me his money bag and then produce a wad of £1 notes from his inside jacket pocket. 'Here you are — straighten these out,' he would say to me.

It was a thrill to count through a lap full of paper money and tell him how much we had taken.

When we reached the isolated gated road through the fields at Dunton, Dad would stop the van and he and I changed places, me behind the driving wheel and he in the passenger seat. Although I was still only 14 or 15 years old he insisted that I learned to drive. There was very little traffic on the roads then. Every Friday I drove the couple of miles through the fields and, long before I was officially old enough, I was a competent driver.

Each Sunday morning the Soulbury orders had to be made up ready for Monday, as well as the tedious job of doing up the rations. Sugar came loose in a sack and was weighed into 1 lb blue paper bags. Where there was one person living alone we had to weigh up 8 ozs. Margarine and compound cooking fat came in large blocks and were cut into 4 ozs and 2 ozs rations. Butter was easier to deal with, at 2 ozs per person. Quarter-pound packets of tea had to be broken open and weighed into 2 ozs per person. Cheese and bacon were also on ration at 4 ozs per person but we did not cut or wrap those until required. Many things were in short supply. Occasionally the wholesaler would let my parents have a flank of fat American streaky bacon, off ration, which my mother boiled in a large pot.

LEFT: Dad — Sergeant Bonner of the Special Constabulary — enjoyed being in the Police Force, especially as his father had been a Chief Superintendent. RIGHT: Charlie Kirk lived in Annie Green's house and was the local taxi man, wireless and bicycle repairer, and in later years newspaper delivery man. BELOW: Floss Kirk, Charlie's wife, taken in 1986.

THE WAR YEARS

Visual signs of the war were not much in evidence in Stoke Hammond.

When they reached the required age young men were called up. Two local girls, Edna Kirk and Freda Williams, joined the ATS. Adults of eligible age were drafted into war work and older residents joined the ARP, Home Guard or special constabulary. Dad joined the 'specials' and loved it. He was proud of his uniform and was soon promoted to sergeant, in charge of special constables in other villages. These he had to meet on point duty to sign their books and record that they were there. When the Royal Train travelled on the main line through Stoke Hammond, Dad had to stand on the railway bridge until it had passed safely. For his work in the special constabulary he was allowed extra petrol coupons.

Some of the villagers worked at the now famous Bletchley Park where, in the most unlikely of Nissen huts, the German Enigma code was successfully broken. No one knew until after the war what went on there.

Evacuees came from the east end of London to live in the village. I vividly remember a crocodile of frightened little children walking past our shop behind Mr Gadsden, the billeting officer. He had been dropping off one here and two there around the houses. I hoped he would bring a couple to our house, but they walked on by. Jean's Mum had two boys named Fred and Raymond billeted on her. They were several years younger than us so we were not that interested. During the winter months however, when I spent evenings at Jean's house we played all sorts of card games and darts together. Some of the unlikeliest householders suddenly found themselves responsible for other people's young children. Even middle-aged couples who had never had any children of their own were allocated one or two.

Once, a convoy of Churchill tanks came rumbling through the village, their heavy tracks squealing and making a deafening noise. I was working in the shop at the time and thought the Germans had invaded without my knowledge! I was even more scared when several pulled to a standstill on the village green and in front of our shop. Out of the tanks jumped young soldiers, who crowded into the shop to buy cigarettes etc. We were packed out and in a dither I did not know who to serve first. With trembling hands and an addled brain I undercharged several of the young men, who grinned at their companions and came back for more. It was only when the terrifyingly noisy tanks had trundled up the hill, having cut up the green with their tracks, that I gathered my wits together and realised what I had done (I did not tell Dad).

My sister was now walking out with a young man whose name was Fred Ritchie. He was the fourth son of a family of seven sons and one daughter. The Ritchie family were farmers and lived opposite us at Tyrells Manor. Tragically, their only daughter Mary died of diphtheria when she was about 12 years old.

Fred was a handsome young man with dark hair and a thin moustache. I was 10 years younger and used to think he looked like the film star Clark Gable. Fred and my sister eventually announced their engagement and married at the Methodist Church in 1941.

Soon after, the Ritchie family moved away from the village to another farm at Astwood in Bedfordshire. For a time my sister and her new husband shared a big farmhouse with his parents until a small cottage became available for them.

My brother Fred was working on the round again with Dad, and I, with the help of Mum, worked in the shop and Post Office.

When we were not at work Jean and I spent all our time together. In the summer we went for long rides on our bicycles. We tended to cycle around the villages in the hope of sighting local boys. On one occasion we had cycled through the villages of Soulbury and Stewkley when, on the outskirts of Wing, we saw two boys leaning on their bikes against a bridge over a brook. As we passed they whistled after us and we, no doubt, gave them the 'come on' signal, because they got on their bikes and began to pedal after us. As they began to catch up we pedalled faster. When we turned towards Liscombe Park, heading for home, they turned too! We flew through Liscombe Park and turned towards Soulbury. About 100 yards behind us — to our consternation — so did they! It was uphill, the road was twisty and turning and our legs felt like lead, but we did not dare ease up. On the other side of Soulbury the road dropped down steeply then rose up and over the railway bridge. We did not bother to apply our brakes but rode at breakneck speed until we reached the main road at the Three Locks (a public house beside the Grand Union Canal). There we turned left towards Stoke Hammond, now only a mile from home. Fortunately, on reaching the Three Locks the two boys applied their brakes, circled in the road and turned back to face the way they had come. We turned in our saddles and, thanking our lucky stars, waved them a cheeky farewell.

Another summer pastime Jean and I enjoyed was playing tennis. Jean's Uncle Tom (from whom we collected the milk) had an only daughter named Gwen, who was several years older than us. At the top of one of his fields, known as Phoebe's Orchard, Mr Simmons had had a tennis court laid down for Gwen and her friends. Because Jean was Gwen's cousin we too were privileged to play. On other occasions Jean and I cycled to Bletchley to play on the public courts in the Central Gardens. The hard courts right in the centre of the town were beautiful, with rose beds close by and seats to sit on. Sadly the tennis courts and gardens have now gone, to make way for a car-park and Leisure Centre.

Besides playing cards and darts during long winter evenings my friend and I were keen knitters. Another pastime which gave us a great deal of pleasure was music. Jean had learned to play the violin and I accompanied her on the piano. We spent many musical evenings playing our favourite pieces and often performed in other churches in concerts organised by our church group. We were never bored.

One day in 1942 it was with great excitement that Jean told me a piece of news in confidence. 'Uncle Jack has sold some of his Dorcas land to the Air Ministry and there's going to be a RAF camp there!' I could not believe my ears. An RAF camp in Stoke Hammond, with all those lovely airmen, surely life would never be the same again!

In due course lots of tall wooden pylons were erected in the fields at Dorcas. Next, some older RAF men came to lodge in the village. They were the riggers who put up wires between the pylons. This was to be a wireless - receiving station, and an important one too. A large Nissen hut was then erected to house the equipment, followed by several smaller huts to accommodate the airmen. But before the camp was ready for occupation something else happened.

Charlie Kirk, our neighbour who lived across the green in what used to be Annie Green's little cottage, was called up into the RAF. He was an older man who ran his own taxi business, sold batteries and charged accumulators for wirelesses. He and his wife Floss had been married for many years but had had no children. Charlie hated the thought of leaving his wife alone while he was away. 'Don't worry,' Dad told him, 'We'll see that she's all right. If she likes, she can come and work in the shop,' he added. Floss did 'like' and came to join the 'firm', where she became almost one of the family and stayed to dinner with us each day.

One morning just after Christmas when she came in to work she confided to me, 'Elsie's got a lodger — he's ever such a nice young man and has got curly hair'. Elsie was her sister-in-law and lived in the village. At 17 and unattached, I pricked up my ears.

Further enquiries established that the 'nice young man' was the new tractor driver at Tyrells Manor Farm and, furthermore, that he liked prunes and custard! I yearned to know more (being partial to prunes and custard myself). Early next morning the shop doorbell rang and in walked a curly-haired young man who I had not seen before. I guessed who it was at once. He came to the Post Office counter and asked for a tuppeny-ha'penny stamp. While he was sticking it on his letter I had a good look at him. He was tall, dark and (in my opinion) handsome and wore a dark green boiler suit.

It did not take long for me to find out that his name was Andrew Aitken. Every morning he came into the shop for a tuppeny-ha'penny stamp and I soon felt at ease talking to him and telling him of things that went on in the village.

'There's a whist drive in the village hall every Friday', I said, 'Why don't you come?' — and the following Friday I met him at the village hall. The next Friday, Andy asked if I would go to the pictures with him.

We met on top of the hill and set off for Bletchley on our bikes. As we cycled along I found out that his home was in Sussex and that his father was farm bailiff on a large estate. He had a younger brother named Hunter and a younger sister called Elizabeth and before her marriage his mother had been a school teacher. Over the next few weeks we went to whist drives, the pictures and for walks together along quiet country lanes.

In early March Andy dropped a bombshell when he told me he was leaving his job at the end of the month as it was not turning out as he had hoped.

'Where are you going then?' I asked. I got another shock for he said 'South Devon', but when he invited me to Sussex to meet his parents he looked at me hopefully. The invitation set my heart racing but I knew I would have to get my parents' permission first. I was 18 and had never been away from home on my own.

The anticipated weekend arrived and Dad took us in his car to Bletchley station to catch the Euston train on our way to the family's cottage at Old House Farm, Turner's Hill, near Haywards Heath.

There I was warmly welcomed, put at my ease, and learnt something of farm life away from Stoke Hammond.

The Aitken family were Anglican and attended Turner's Hill Church on Sundays. Andy and Hunter when younger had been choirboys there. On Sunday morning I was asked if I would like to go to church.

The lovely old church was perched on the hill and had a commanding view of the rolling South Downs. The service was different from our Methodist one. I did however enjoy the pipe organ music and was envious of the beautiful instrument.

After lunch Andy and I had to think about getting back to Stoke Hammond. Mr and Mrs Aitken took us to the station in their car and saw us off from the platform. The weekend had flown by.

By the end of the week Andy had packed his belongings and was on his way to South Devon.

Meanwhile, back in the village, the young airmen had taken up residence at the wireless station. They came into the shop for cigarettes and stamps so I was able to tell Jean all about them. A few came to the weekly whist drive and, when a dance was held in the village hall, it was pleasant to have different partners, but I kept faith with Andy — if anyone asked me for a date my stock phrase was, 'I don't think my boyfriend would like it!'

We got to know some of the boys really well because several of them came regularly to the evening service at Chapel. After the service Auntie Win (Mum's youngest sister) invited them and us around to her house for hymn singing around the piano. I would play everyone's favourite hymns. We had a real choir going and used to let rip! I don't know how she managed it out of her rations, but my aunt provided tea and spam sandwiches for us all.

One morning towards the end of 1943 my expected letter arrived from Andy and in it he told me he had received a letter from his mother telling him there was a vacancy at Old House Farm for a tractor driver — and that he was going to take it. For some time he had realised how isolated he felt living in Devon. With this in mind he had handed in his notice and was moving back to live with his parents. By early December Andy had settled back in Sussex and I went to spend Christmas with the Aitken family.

This photograph shows part of the new estate built on Phoebe's Orchard where in summer we used to play tennis on Mr T. Simmons' grass court.

ABOVE: The RAF Wireless Station at Stoke Hammond was at Dorcas on this site; here the buildings and pylons used to stand. BELOW: Dorcas Lane in springtime; it led to the RAF Camp.

LEFT: Young Margaret Bonner aged 17 years. RIGHT: The young Andy Aitken. BELOW: The newly-built cottage at Old House Farm, Sussex where Andy Aitken's family lived, and, right, the cottage where Andy and the author began married life.

ABOVE: Andy Aitken on the motor bike on which the author rode pillion from Sussex to Bucks. BELOW: A young Andy Aitken, right, working on the farm with his father and younger brother, Hunter.

HERE AND THERE

In 1944 Andy came up to spend Christmas with us at Stoke Hammond and on my twentieth birthday we became engaged. The following year we were married at the Methodist Church and then we moved into the farm cottage adjoining Andy's parents' home in Sussex.

Every few weeks we went home to spend the weekend in Stoke Hammond with Mum and Dad. It was wonderful to see them and catch up with all the local news. It made me realise even more how I missed being at the centre of village life. The journey to Buckinghamshire on the pillion seat of Andy's motorbike was literally a pain in the backside.

Each time we returned to Sussex I became more and more reluctant to leave Stoke Hammond. Of course, I loved Andy dearly and our cottage home, but I sorely missed working in the village shop overlooking the green. I missed all the chit-chat with customers. I missed Friday night whist drives and Saturday night dances. I missed attending the Methodist Church twice on a Sunday and all the social activities that went with it.

Most days I wrote long letters to Mum, which she answered promptly because she knew how lonely I was. There is no doubt that I was home-sick for Stoke Hammond, and Andy knew it too.

The first year of our marriage was eventful. During the summer months visitors stayed with us. Mum, Dad and Fred came and so did Jean. Since my marriage, she had found a steady boyfriend, Don Tooth. He had attended Bletchley School when we were there. Two more friends were Peter Venn and his girlfriend Norma Gadsden from Stoke Hammond.

Early in June my sister told me that after five years of marriage she was expecting her first baby in January. In mid-June Grandpa Scott was taken ill. On 2 July 1946 he died in Northampton Hospital. When the funeral arrangements had been made I travelled home alone to Stoke Hammond. The service was held in the Methodist Church where he and all the Scotts had always attended. Grandpa was laid to rest in the churchyard up the road with his beloved wife Sarah, who had died two years earlier.

It was mid-January and the time was imminent for Annis to give birth, and I set off for Buckinghamshire. Before I arrived snow began to fall heavily and quickly settled. It continued overnight and all next day, making travelling almost impossible. My sister went into labour and Doctor Morphy and the mid-wife were sent for.

Not long ago I visited my doctor's group practice and what a busy place it was, half a dozen doctors occupying half a dozen rooms. As many receptionists worked behind the desk, making appointments, while the practice nurse was busy in her room with a queue of people waiting to see her. In the various waiting areas fractious babies rested feverish rosy cheeks on anxious Mums' shoulders. Frail old folk waited patiently. My mind went back to my childhood days and to how our medical needs in the villages were met then.

Our family was attended by Dr Frank Morphy, and later by his son, Dr Brian. 'Old' Dr Morphy first came to the village when he was quite a young man and cared for my grandparents, my parents, myself and my family. He was greatly respected and loved by all his patients. My grandmother thought the world of him and once knitted a long woolly scarf to put around his neck when he was called out at night.

When I was about 10 years old I was ill with quinsies. My throat was so inflamed and swollen that it almost closed. Dr Morphy came to visit me morning and evening for some time. He prescribed hot salt-bags to be tied around my neck by means of a woolly sock. The bags were bulky and uncomfortable and as it was summertime the heat added to my discomfort. The only bright aspect of the whole episode was that I was prescribed ice and ice-cream to suck.

I never knew Dr Morphy to be in a hurry or annoyed for being summoned and cannot recall him having a day off or ever refusing to come for a home visit when asked. Dr Morphy was not only a physician, but a friend, and it was he who attended Annis when she gave birth to David.

Movement on the roads and railways all over the country was almost at a standstill, still in the grip of arctic weather. Severe frost and snow continued for six weeks. I stayed on at Stoke Hammond.

ABOVE: Mr and Mrs Aitken outside their retirement cottage at Soulbury. BELOW: Andy Aitken in the Park in 1947.

ABOVE: Mr Tom Goodman, right, and his young son John work on the allotment. BELOW: Orchard Cottage, opposite the Anglican Church, where Mr and Mrs Harry Keen lived.

HOME FROM HOME

It was only a matter of time before Andy realised I would never be happy living in Sussex. My ties with Stoke Hammond were much too strong. We were always in close contact with my family and knew all that went on in the village.

One day a letter arrived from my mother telling us that four houses were being built and that one was to be reserved for an agricultural worker. The farmer allocated the house was Edgar Venn, who lived at Dorcas and was looking for a general farm worker. At dinnertime I put Mum's letter on the table for my husband to read and watched his face.

'Well,' I said, before he had hardly finished, 'How about applying?' He did not say he would, and he did not say he would not, but after I had hammered away all through dinner he was convinced that nothing in the whole wide world would make me happier than to move back to Stoke. In the end he had little option but to agree to apply.

Mr Venn confirmed that Andy could have the job and that when the new house was finished it would be allocated to us. There was just one snag — he needed his farmworker to begin as soon as possible. To my mind this was a plus rather than a minus. The sooner we moved the better!

Once again my parents rallied around and said we could stay with them until the house was ready. After telling his parents of our intentions Andy gave in his notice at Old House Farm and we made arrangements to move back. On 8 June 1948, 15 months after our marriage, our furniture was unloaded into shop premises again. This was home — not home with my parents, but home in the community and village. As our belongings were arranged in my old room, the piano took up its original position in the front room.

It was easy to slip back into village life. Andy cycled to and from the farm and came home to dinner at midday. I helped in the house, shop and Post Office. The customers, my friends, told me all the local news and made me feel involved again. In the evenings Andy and I joined in village social life. We attended the Young People's League and took part in quizzes, debates and spelling-bees. Our group of young people also gave concerts around the local churches. I joined the Women's Institute and formed a choir which visited local old people's homes to entertain. Andy and I became members of the Methodist Church and I took over training the children for Sunday School Anniversary services — what a contrast to the lonely life in Sussex!

Although Andy had always been a farmworker, our ambition was to rent a smallholding of our own. At that time the County Council owned a number of these small farms and periodically one became vacant. Several times we applied but without success. Then the day dawned when some land on the outskirts of the village, known as the Allotment Field, came onto the market. It belonged to Harry Keen, who lived at Orchard Cottage opposite the church, and comprised seven acres. Dad bought the land on our behalf and gave it to us as a step on the ladder towards our own farm. Part of the field was divided into strips of land and was owned and used by villagers as gardens. Cecil Harrup had the first two. We owned the next patch, consisting of a closely packed orchard of apple trees and a sleeper-built barn. The next two strips belonged to Mr Shepherd — the railway delivery man — then there was a strip belonging to my cousin, Harold Scott. Adjoining his was Mr Goodman's piece and next to him came Uncle Jim's two pieces. On the opposite side of the field was another apple orchard and there were several more barns. Without delay we bought some hens and an in-calf cow from a local dealer. In time she produced a black calf and Andy went to market and bought two more for the cow to suckle. While he was at work on the farm I kept an eye on the livestock, fed and watered the hens and collected the eggs.

Among those who knew that Andy and I one day hoped to rent a Council smallholding were Mr and Mrs Gadsden, who lived in the village at Grove Farm, with their four daughters and one son. Mr Gadsden was a County Councillor and headed numerous committees. When harvest time came around that year he offered me a job on the farm, driving his tractor from field to rickyard with loads of corn. With trepidation and dressed in khaki bib and brace overalls, I went to work. The tractor — a big blue Fordson Major — looked a monster to me. The bonnet covering the huge engine made me realise just how powerful it was, especially as I had been used to driving Dad's Austin Ten. A large trailer with ladders attached to the front and back was secured behind the tractor.

I climbed into the driving seat and a local man named Harry French and the under-cowman, Henry Ogden, climbed up beside me. I started the engine, opened the throttle, let out the clutch and we were off. It was anything but a comfortable ride as we bumped our way to the cornfield. 'Drive along the rows of stooks,' I was told. At the end of the row I had to turn around. 'Do a figure of eight,' the men instructed me. After a few ends I got the hang of it and managed to be facing in the right direction for the next row. Henry was an expert loader and made the job look easy. Up and up went the sheaves until the load towered above me. When it was about 15 feet high a rope from the back to front ladders secured it. Now it was my responsibility to get it safely back to the farmyard. Harry and Henry jumped onto the tractor, one on either side of me. I opened the throttle a little, let out the clutch and moved at a slow walking pace. The huge load creaked and rocked from side to side as the wheels went into ruts. I was terrified it would fall off! 'You'll have to go faster than that,' the men urged me, 'they're waiting to unload in the rickyard!' With my heart in my mouth, I opened up the throttle a little more and we moved along swaying from side to side. Somehow or other I arrived safely with the load still intact where Mr Gadsden was waiting to build the rick on the straw base he had prepared. The full trailer was unhitched beside the base, an empty trailer attached to the tractor I was driving and off we went again for another load.

Another seasonal job that came my way was threshing. I did not actually have anything to do with the corn, my job being on the baler dealing with the straw. I had to thread long, black, grease-coated wires between the bales to the other side of the baler where another man threaded them back to me between the next bale. I then had to secure the ends through loops in the wire by twisting it several times with my fingers. But the worst thing of all was the choking black dust that exploded in my face every time the metal plates compressed the straw. When we left off at lunchtime on that first day I was absolutely filthy. My face, hair and clothes hung with black dust. Not only that, the dust had settled in my lungs so that I could not take a deep breath.

A less disagreeable although back-aching job was potato lifting. Mr Gadsden grew quite a large acreage of potatoes, which he ploughed out of the ground row by row. With big buckets 'our gang' picked them up and tipped them into sacks, in which they were transported back to the farm.

Andy was still working for Mr Venn at Dorcas Farm and between us we were able to save a few pounds. The council houses were nearing completion but, as we now owned a piece of land, we decided to apply to the County Council for a licence to build an agricultural dwelling. This was granted without any objections so we turned down the house.

In June 1949, a year after our return to the village, plans had been drawn up and passed for our bungalow and the builder had pegged out the foundations in the Allotment Field close to the road. My parents lent us the money to build, to be paid back as and when we could afford it.

To speed things along, Andy volunteered to dig the foundations. So after work and at the weekends we worked as a team. No foundations were ever dug with such love, precision and care as ours, but there was great satisfaction in a job well done.

We watched impatiently as the builders laid each row of bricks. The walls began to grow until window frames appeared, carpenters hammered on the roof trusses and battens for the tiles, and tilers started work.

As winter approached, in the evenings Andy and I would light the Raeburn with offcuts of wood left by the carpenters and burn up rotten boughs from the old apple trees. The main electricity supply stopped at the railway bridge so it did not reach our bungalow. We had a Tilley lamp that ran on paraffin and had to be pumped up to maintain the pressure. How happy we were sitting on a wooden sawing-horse enjoying the warmth and privacy of *our* home!

Just before Christmas 1949 the bungalow was finished and before the New Year had arrived we moved our furniture again, this time into 'Fairfields'.

Who could ask for more? I had tasted life away from Stoke Hammond village and hated the flavour! Now I vowed that, if I had my way, never again would I be separated from the village where I was born. Nearly 50 years later, the village has grown, much has changed, and new names replace the old, yet it is still the same place, and I still have that same sense of belonging. Stoke Hammond is our home.

Bluebell the cow, with her black calf, watched by the author. In the background is her newly built bungalow, named Fairfields.

ABOVE: Mr Tom Goodman takes a breather on the allotment gate. BELOW: Mr Gadsden's tractor and trailer with a high load, similar to the one the author drove.

INDEX

All figures in *italics* refer to illustrations.

Adams, Fred 19,*22*
Adcock, Gill *7*
Anglican Church 21,*26,27,*
    51,66
Aitken, Andrew.......*69,75,80,*
    84,85,*87,88,*89,*91,*93,94,96
    Elizabeth.........................84
    Hunter.....................84,*88*
    Mr & Mrs 84,*91*
allotment field 94,95
Andrews, Stan..............*2,*60
Anniversary celebrations,
    Sunday School 60,61,65,
    66,67,93
ARP................................81
Astwood 82
Attendance Officer 50
ATS...................................81
Australia 45
Aylesbury 79
barges 32,33
Barron family *45,51,*69
    Arthur 11,67,*68,*69
    George *35*
Bletchley....9,11,21,22,31,46,
    67,77,83,84
    Junction 11,19
    Park 81
    School 89
    Station 84
Bone, Arthur 20
    George *56*,59
Bonner, Annis 45,47,77,
    78,82,89
    Bert.......32,45,46,47,60,*63,*
    67,73,77,78,79,*80,*81,82,
    83,89,94
    Fred 45,47,*57,75,*82,89
    Harry 45
    Margaret.........................87
Bragenham Side 20,31,32
Bridge Farm 20,*20*
brook *30,*31,*33,*74
Brook Farm 20,*23,33*
Burcott......................46,78
Bushell, Len *8*
Canal, Grand Union....20,32,
    *37,43,*62
Capp, Mrs Harold 78,79
carol singing 67
Central Gardens 83
Chadwell Farm 21
Chambers, Mrs *69*

Chapel Yard 9,*53*
Cheshire, Mrs H. *69*
choir, WI.....................73,93
Church Road 21,*34,*66
Churchill tanks 81,82
Collins, F. *75*
Collyer, Ethel....................*25*
Common Farm 21
commuters, London 22
concerts 60,73,83
Co-op................................77
council houses 9,20,*43,*45,
    49,95
Cowlishaws........................77
Cox, Guy and John............*68*
cricket 49,74,75
Dairy Farm 22,31,67
dancing classes 73
Darkie.........................46,47
Denchfield, D. *75*
dentist, school..................50
Dixon's Garage..................78
Dolphin Inn........*37,*67,*72,*74
Dorcas Farm 21,83,*86,*
    93,94
    Lane.......................21,*86*
drama group.....................73
Drayton Parslow 21,46,*63,*
    73,78
Dunton 46,47,79
Durrell, Wilfred 60
evacuees...........................81
Fairfields....................*96,*96
farming 19,*53,54,*94
Fenny Road 45
    Stratford 77
fishermen..........................33
floods 20,22,31,*34*
football 49
Fountaine, Mr 21,*26*
French, Harry..............94,95
Gadsden, Mr & Mrs...........21,
    *28,29,*69,81,94,95,*97*
    Norma 89
Gale, Mr & Mrs Frank..*16,*20
    Robert............................20
Garner, Bill............32,*41,43*
ghosts...............................*28*
Goodman, Tom and
    John.................*92,*94,*97*
Great Brickhill..................73
Green, The 9,*16,*31,*34,*49,
    *53,*81
    Annie 7,9,83
Grove Farm 21,*28,29,*94

Cottage *34,35*
Gurney, Mr & Mrs
    Andrew 21
Gurr, Mrs..........................79
Harrup, Cecil..........32,*37,38,*
    *41,*94
harvest *55,70,*94
Haywards Heath................84
Hill, The...........................49
Holmes, George 20
    Mr 20
Home Guard 81
Ivy Cottage *34*
Jacobs Dairy......................45
Keen, Harry.................*91,*94
    Joe 11
    Mrs M. *69*
King, Mrs..........................*64*
Kirk, Arthur.......*18,*19,31,49,
    55,67
    Charlie *80,*83
    Edna 81
    Floss *80,*83
    Raymond *2*
    Tom 11,*18,*19,31,49,67
Laurels, The 21,*26*
Leighton Buzzard.....9,19,22,
    60,61,73,78
Leisure Centre, Bletchley..83
Line, Mr & Mrs Charlie.....21
Liscombe Park..................82
Little London 76,798
    Thatch...........................*17*
lock-keepers...32,*38,*40,*41,43*
London 22,81
Lovatt, Mr.........................60
Methodist Chapel....*53,*62,65,
    66,67,*69,70,*71,73,82,85,
    89,93
Milton Keynes 9,22
Moat Farm....*18,*19,*30,*31,45,
    49,74
mobile shop ...60,*63,*77,78,79
Morphy, Dr Brian..............90
    Dr Frank........................89,90
Mount Pleasant...19,20,22,*30*
Munro, Miss 50,51,52
Murphy, K. *75*
Newton Longville 21,46,78
    Road 9,21,*56,*59
nit nurse 50
Northampton 9,89
Ogden, Henry 94,95
Old House Farm....84,85,*87*
Rectory *28*

98

Olde Bell Close............*16,17*
Inn *24*
One Lock.....................*32,37*
Orchard Cottage *91*,94
organ, Chapel.....51,52,56,65
Oriel Cinema......................78
Oving........................*46*,79
Papermill Farm *20,22*
paraffin round ...45,46,47,60,
79
Parish Council 74
parson...........................50,51
pavilion..............................74
Penny, Charles 22
Ernie...........................21
Phillips family....................21
Phoebe's Orchard....*33*,83,*85*
piano lessons 51,52
playing field.......................47
pond, village..............31,*34*
Post Office 77,78,82,83,93
potato lifting.....................95
pump, village...........31,*35,36*
Pump House......................*40*
Purrett, Miss 78
Purrett's Music Shop 78
RAF............................83,85,*86*
rag-and-bone man.........61,62
railway, LMS......10,11,*11*,19,
22,74,81
rations..............................79
Rectory Farm.....................22
Rice, Billy and Emma..12,59,
60,*63*,74
Richardson, John 21
Ritchie, David...................90
Fred 82
Mary 82
roadmen 59
Robinson, Nell..............65,67
Reg 65
Rodex coat factory.............77
Rose Bank...................10,*12*
Rose Brook Cottage ..9,*13,34*
Royal Train.......................81
Saint Luke's *26,27*

School, Stoke Hammond..20,
45,50,51,*51,52,53,56,57*,74
Scott, Arthur 11
Bess..............................*8*,45
Brian..............................*68*
Elizabeth.......*8*,11,45,46,47
Enid 9,10,12,*13*,59
Florence.....11,46,47,62,77,
78,82,89,93
Fred 11
Frederick and Sarah......*10,
13*
George and Daisy.....11,*13*,
20,45
Grandma ...10,*14*,45,51,*54*,
89,90
Grandpa 9,10,11,45,49,
51,*54*,65,89
Harold *8*,45,94
Jim and Emma 12,*13,16*,
58,59,65,94
John *29*,66
Madge...........................*13*
Minnie 11,*14*
Will and Vi..................9,*13*
Winifred................11,20,85
Shackshaft, A. and G. *75*
Sharpe, Mr & Mrs
Albert........................11,77
Shepherd, Frank 10
Ivy.................................20
Les................................10
Mr & Mrs 10,19,49,94
shop, old.....................*8,9,13*
new 7,11,32,45,46,49,60,
77,78,81,82,83,85,93
Simmons, Ethel 21
George.................7,9,21,81
Gwen..........................82,83
Jack...........................21,83
Jean.......10,*12*,21,52,61,*62*,
65,73,77,81,82,83,85,89
Kate 21
Tom and Elsie 20,*23*,47,
82,83,*85*
Will 20

Slads, The.....................31,49
social evenings....................73
Soulbury ...20,46,47,78,79,82
Albert............................59
South Devon 84,85
Southlands....................21,67
special constabulary...........81
Spoil Bank 21
Stanesby family *75*
Stewkley..............*46*,47,60,82
Stoke House 67
Lodge 71
Sunday School *58*,60,61,
65,66,67,*68*,93
Sussex 84,85,89,93
Swan Cottage....................*29*
swingbridge 32,*42*
Three Locks............32,*39,43*
Public House.........47,*49*,82
threshing 95
Tibbles, Mr 61
Tofield, Mrs......................45
Tooth, Don 89
Turner's Hill.....................84
Church..........................84
Turnover bridge 20,32,*37*
Tyrells Manor 20,*25*,82,83
Venn, Edgar *93*,95
Peter..............................89
village hall 53,*70,72,73*,74
84,85
visiting traders..............60,61
wells 31,32
Wesleyan Chapel 9
whist drives..............73,84,85
Whitaker, Doris 61,66
Whitchurch 46,47,76,79
White, Mr 60
Wickstead Park 65,66
Williams, Daphne *62*
Freda 81
Wing 46,60,76,78,82
Women's Institute....*72,73*,93
World War II 20,77,81,82,
83,85
Young People's League 93

SUBSCRIBERS

Presentation Copies

1 Stoke Hammond Parish Council
2 Aylesbury Vale District Council
3 Stoke Hammond Methodist Chapel
4 Margaret & Andy Aitken
5 Clive & Carolyn Birch

6 Gillian Jaynes
7 Judith Newman
8 Alison Davies
9 Mr & Mrs Heard
10 Janet Burke
11 Mrs D. Mason
12 Esther L. Smith
13 Anne P. Ambler
14 K.M. Willoughby
15 J.L. Tucker
16 Mrs D. Scott
17 Mr & Mrs K. Breedon
18 Daniel Andrew Donnelly
19 Mrs Elizabeth Davies
20 J. Harmer
21
22 Margaret Davies
23 M. & D. Stanesby
24 Mrs F.M. Elliot
25 Margaret Stanesby
26 R.J. Kirk
27 M.R. Gadsden
28 P. Brown
29 V.J. Scott
30 Audrey Dawson
31 Margaret Phillips
32 Gwen Phillips
33 Salsbury-Potter
34 Nancy Mercy
35 I.V. Robinson
36 Ron Oates & Diane Brown
37 M. Walduck
38 Mrs J. Horner
39 Chris & Gloria Perry
40 N. Little
41
42 Gwen Simmons
43
44 Mrs S. Robson
45 Jackie Tooth

46 Mrs B.M. Smith
47 Mrs P. Linney
48 H. Stratford
49 Judy & Duncan Griffiths
50 David Kessler
51 Colin Dimmock
52 L.C. Weldon
53 Miss J. Simmons
54
55 E.T. Stanley
56 Mrs Edgar J. Venn
57
58 Mrs J. Bone
59
60 W.H. Rees
61 J.A. Cunningham
62 Bucks County Reference Library
63
64 A. Yorke
65
66 Mrs N. Kirk
67
68 Mrs Edna Bates
69 C. Ritchie
70
71 Mrs Rosemary Joyner
72 Geoff Bunyan
73 D.E. Hallwood
74 Isobel Smith-Cresswell
75 A. Willis
76 Mrs M. Leonard
77 Ingrid & Graham Ross
78 Eileen North
79 Trixie Gillham
80 Mrs Sylvia Smale
81 R. Woodcock
82 Mrs V. Redbart
83 R. Kirk
84 Marion Barnell

85 P.W. Bone
86 Graham A. Hallwood
87 Olive Saunders
88 Anthony John Robinson
89 Mrs E.M. Swift
90 Ira Chalmers
91 S. Stonell
92 Betty Shaw
93 G.R. Stanesby
94 M. Rose
95 Tony & Karen Scott
96 Mrs M.A. White
97 Mrs P.M. Paxton
98 Roger J. Colby
99 D.F. Ritchie
100 L. Pearson-Smith
101 Sheila M. Stanesby
102 L.T. Marsh
103 Mrs J. Scott
104 Philip Wheeler
105 Marian Gurney
106 Krystyna Brown
107 Collette Mitchell
108 Mrs Marion Curtis
109 A.D. Mgano
110 G. Christopher
111 Helen Thompson
112 Sheila Hyde
113
114 Mrs Edna Embra
115 Mrs D.R. Atkins
116 Mrs V. Back
117 M.J. Chappell
118 W.H. & E.L. Chappell
119 Bill Farmer
120 B. Arnold
121 Rev Ian Banks
122 Maureen E. Berrett
123 Derek Fletcher
124 Mrs Doreen M. Hankins

125 Mrs M. Chappell	181 Frederick D. Young	237 P. Ritchie
126 The Kellett Family	182 A. Davis	238 R. Beasley
127 Molly West	183 E. Burling	239 Judith Price
128 Pamela Smith	184 Margaret (Madge)	240 Mrs F. Harpin
129 Bill Kirk	185 Cowell	241 Mrs R. Richardson
130 Angela Richardson	186 Mrs F. Harrison	242 Wilf Wheeler
131 Jennifer Mathews	187 Peter R. Garner	243 Richard Faulkner
132 Jill Kirk	188 D. Barker	244 Mrs D.B. Pearce
133 Sue Kirk	189 Marjorie Sharman	245 K.T. Gadsden
134 Richard Kirk	190 Heather Ritchie	246
135 Mrs M. King	191 J. & D. Roads	247 Joyce Smith
136 Mrs J.A. Clare	192 Mrs M.D. Holmes	248 Marjorie Grace
137 Richard Tattam	193	249 Andrea Willey
138 Mr & Mrs G. Cox	194 B. Amos	250 Herb & Connie Willey
139 Mr & Mrs Honeychurch	195 J. Ealing	
	196 H. O. Allen	251287 Buckinghamshire
140 Mrs L. West	197 D. & D.W. Jaynes	- County Library
141 K.E. Parker	198 Davina Swain	255 Service
142 H.T. Wright	199 John Hancock	256 Philip Hanlon
143	200 Doris Goodman	257 Miss E. Winn
144 Hazel Turner	201 Alan Scott	258 Peter Brown
145	202 June Williams	259 A.G. Keddie
146- The Stevenson	203 Mrs U.M. Plumley	260 Mark Flack
148 Family	204 Mrs G. Harlow	261 D. Sharkey
149 Mrs D. Green	205 R.F. Shepherd	262 F.J. Keen
150 Pearl Grice	206 G. Clay	263 Nichola Dancer
151 Stephanie Andrews	207 Joan E. Oswald	264 Christina Honnor
152 Margaret Challis	208 D.E. Higgs	265 Joan Gregory
153 Gerald Denchfield	209 Fred & Dorothy Breeze	266 Mrs Wendy Percy
154 Derek Denchfield		267 Robert James French
155 Janet Deeley	210 Mrs C.G. Gurney	268 Garth & Evelyn Holman
156 J. Clark	211	
157 Dot Parsons	212 Norma Smallridge	269 Irene Mann
158 D. Dimmock	213 Derek John Simmons	270 P.R. Webb
159 D.C. Bonner	214 Mrs D.M. Capp	271 Kathie Doughty
160 L.E. Shepherd	215 Deirdre Kay	272 Mrs M. Coxall
161 June Garner	216 Mrs Vera Quinn	273 Val Farnell
162	217 M. Coward	274 Simon & Julia Walker
163 M. Bonner	218 Fred & Hazel Hearn	275 Brenda Price
164	219 Mrs M. Willett	276 Mrs Gillian Campbell
165 B. Mulcuck	220 K. Shackshaft	277 John Bowler
166 Mr & Mrs S. Johannes	221 Mrs Joan Ogden	278 Flo Scott
	222 Mrs A. Lusher	279 Mrs Smale
167 Mr & Mrs D. Creighton	223 Florence M. Pollard	280 Mrs E. Baker
	224 Mrs N. Salisbury	281 Mrs D'Agostino
168 D.J. Edwards	225 Mrs M.L. Noy	282 Stephen Andrews
169 Lilian Ingram	226 B.S. Sisley	283 R.F. Dickens
170 Doreen French	227 Mrs T. Brown	284
172 D.J. Tufano	228 H. Hearn	285 Sally & Steve Lerkouskise
173 J.T.R. Phillips	229 R.J. & M.A. Broome	
174 Mrs J.E. Fullard	230 Mrs L. Houghton	286 M.E. Lambourne
175 Mrs J.A. Heaton	231 R.J. Harrup	287 Timothy Jaynes
176 Mrs M.P. Dancer	232 Mrs M.L. Knight	288 Gemma Jaynes
177 Mrs S.G. Wood	233 Mrs F. Bickle	289 Philippa Jaynes
178 A. Wood	234 Marily & Paul Dodd	
179 T. Scott	235 Ann Ford	
180 A. Seaman	236 Nancy Perkins	*Remaining names unlisted*